I0816580

Also by the Author

Just Tyrus
Nuff Said

WHAT IT IS, AMERICA

Tyrus

A POST HILL PRESS BOOK
ISBN: 979-8-89565-212-1
ISBN (eBook): 979-8-89565-213-8

Cover design by Conroy Accord

This book, as well as any other Post Hill Press publications, may be purchased in bulk quantities at a special discounted rate. Contact orders@posthillpress.com for more information.

All people, locations, events, and situations are portrayed to the best of the author's memory. While all of the events described are true, many names and identifying details have been changed to protect the privacy of the people involved.

Post Hill Press
New York • Nashville
posthillpress.com

Published in the United States of America
2 3 4 5 6 7 8 9 10

To my children for always inspiring me to do more, work harder, and be better, so that they can have the best opportunity to live the American dream.

To my wife, Ingrid. Thank you for fourteen years of love and loyalty, and supporting my drive to be a provider for my family. You're beautiful, smart, and devoted to me and our family. Thank you for all your sacrifices.

TABLE OF CONTENTS

FOREWORD BY PRESIDENT DONALD J. TRUMP

I HAVE KNOWN GEORGE "TYRUS" Murdoch for many years. Throughout his career in Professional Wrestling and Television, he has earned the respect and admiration of millions. While Late Night Television Ratings have rapidly declined, Tyrus continues to be a STAR, using his iconic Wit and Humor to target the Radical Democrats, and their joyless campaign against the American Way of Life, Liberty, and the Pursuit of Happiness.

After doing hundreds of Radio and Television interviews throughout the course of the 2024 Presidential Election, one of the highlights for me was stopping by the set of *Gutfeld!*, just a few weeks prior to Election Day. There is something special about this cast of characters and, on that occasion, they did not disappoint. Tyrus even designed a custom "TRUMP 2024" Championship belt, which he presented to me. I knew then, he was diehard "MAGA!"

In the following pages, Tyrus tells the true story of the 2024 Presidential Election, with his own unique insights, strongly rooted in Common Sense and Love for our Country. Joe Biden, Kamala Harris, and their friends on the Extreme Left still do not understand what "MAGA" means, but Tyrus, and the Majority across our Nation do, which is why we won the Most Important Election in the History of our Country, with Victory in all seven Swing States, 312 Electoral Votes, and the Popular Vote by a lot!

Tyrus has always been a Great Fighter, who will never let you down. This Book is fantastic—Enjoy!

—*President Donald J. Trump*

AUTHOR'S NOTE

THIS BOOK, IN MY OPINION, goes hard on Joe Biden and the people in his circle who gaslit America for four long years—not just about his physical condition but about various aspects of his presidency and the decisions made under his watch.

As I was nearing the completion of the first draft of this manuscript, the news broke that former President Biden had been diagnosed with a very serious case of prostate cancer. Now, let me be clear: I wish the president no harm. It's a tragic diagnosis, and my heart goes out to him and his family during this difficult time. I believe that everyone deserves compassion, especially when facing health challenges.

However, I want to emphasize that this serious health issue has no bearing on the criticisms laid out in this book. The reality is that if there was knowledge of his condition that was hidden from the American people, it only adds another layer to the massive cover-ups surrounding his presidency. Transparency should be the name of the game in leadership, and any failure to disclose such critical information raises serious questions about trust and accountability.

Right now, I don't have all the answers, and I can't claim to know the full reality of his health situation. What I do know is that regardless of his personal struggles, his administration needs to be held accountable for what I believe to be one of the greatest presidential scandals in history. The actions taken during his time in office have had profound impacts on our nation, and we cannot allow personal circumstances to overshadow the need for accountability.

So, while I extend my well wishes to him and his family, I will keep those sentiments separate from my belief that our leaders must answer for their decisions. Compassion and accountability can coexist, and it's crucial that we demand the latter while also acknowledging the humanity of those involved.

At the end of the day, this book is about the truth—the good, the bad, and the ugly. And the truth is that we, as a nation, deserve better.

INTRODUCTION

IN A WORLD SATED WITH noise, where opinions are flung like confetti at a parade, I've always believed that the most crucial thing we can do is listen to one another. That's it. My journey as a commentator on Fox News and a stand-up comic has taken me across this great country, where I've encountered people from diverse backgrounds. It's through these encounters that I have come to appreciate the power of conversation—the raw, unfiltered dialogue that happens when you step off the stage and engage with your fellow Americans.

Let me take you back to a particularly memorable experience that sparked the inspiration for this book: my first encounter with Donald Trump on *Gutfeld!*, the Greg Gutfeld show. The taping came together in a whirlwind; we found out just three days prior that I'd be sharing the stage with the former president. Nerves were high, excitement buzzing through the air like static electricity. My mindset was simple: regardless of who the guest was, I had to be the star of my own performance. After all, this was my house, and I was determined to make it a show for the ages.

When Trump arrived, I was struck by the palpable energy in the studio. He entered the room like a whirlwind, commanding attention as if he were the headliner in a sold-out arena. After a brief handshake, we dove into a conversation that felt as natural as a late-night jam session with friends.

He joked about his reputation, teasingly proclaiming, "I'm not just muscle; I've got brains, too!" I smirked and reminded him, "Don't worry, kid; if you get out there, just lean on me. I got you." The laughter that followed eased the tension in the room, and I could see the audience leaning in, captivated.

What struck me most was how he engaged with the crowd, his charisma igniting a fire that set the audience ablaze. When the announcement was made that he would be on the show instead of Michelle Tafoya, the collective gasp was almost deafening, followed by a raucous cheer. It was a reminder of just how deeply he resonates with everyday Americans—a connection I had a hunch would pay off in the upcoming 2024 election.

Now, the show itself was a mix of humor and genuine moments. But it also had its fair share of hilarity behind the scenes. I distinctly remember Greg asking me to switch seats right before the show started. Picture this: I'm all set to take my place, and Greg casually suggests, "Hey, why don't you sit between the president and the audience?" I raised an eyebrow and shot back, "So you want me to sit between the crowd and the president, who's just had two assassination attempts? Am I hearing this right?" Greg nervously laughed, and I couldn't help but think, "Well, there are worse ways to go!" It was a comedic moment that set the tone for the evening—one that reminded me that even in the most serious situations, laughter can be a powerful tool.

As the show progressed, Trump displayed a knack for self-deprecation. Then came the moment that truly turned the tide of the evening. Wanting to show my appreciation for Trump, I decided to present him with my own custom championship belt. The gold belt was emblazoned with "Trump

2024" on the front, proudly showcasing Fox's support for his campaign. I could feel the anticipation in the air as I handed it to him.

"Thank you for WrestleMania IV and V, by the way," I said, referencing the iconic events held at Trump Plaza in Atlantic City. "Thank you very much. But if you're going to sit in that chair, if you're going to do the Tyrus experience, you have to do it right. Because you are the people's champion, Mr. Trump."

His eyes lit up as he examined the belt, and I could see the genuine surprise on his face. "Wow, this is heavy!" he exclaimed. "This is a real one!"

I couldn't help but chuckle and shot back, "Like I'm gonna give a fake belt to the next president of the United States!" The room erupted in laughter, and in that moment, it felt like we were all part of something special. It wasn't just a belt; it was a symbol of solidarity, a nod to the entertainment world we both inhabited, and a testament to the unique connection we shared.

Trump held the belt like a true champion, and I could see the energy shift in the room. It was a moment that captured the spirit of the show and the man himself. This was not just politics; it was an acknowledgment of the bond forged between a former wrestling champion and a sitting president, both larger-than-life figures in their own right.

The belt presentation became a viral sensation. Clips of him donning the belt and flexing his muscles circulated across social media like wildfire. Memes and gifs popped up faster than you could say, "Make America Great Again." The imagery of Trump, the political powerhouse, combined with the over-the-top flair of pro wrestling struck a chord that resonated with his base and beyond. It was a perfect encapsulation of the night: a celebration of personality, humor, and the spirit of the fight.

But the real magic happened after the cameras stopped rolling. Following the taping, Trump took the time to engage with my daughter, Georgie, for nearly twenty minutes. Picture this: a former president, sitting down on a couch, laughing and chatting with a little girl as if they were old pals. It was heartwarming to witness. He asked her questions, listened intently, and made her feel like the most important person in the room, much like he would with his own grandkids. In an age where politicians often rush past the people they serve, here was Trump—consistent and authentic—taking the time to ensure everyone had their moment with him.

I couldn't help but think how rare it is to find that kind of sincerity in a political figure. Unlike any other politician I've encountered, Trump was no different once the cameras stopped rolling. He remained engaged, warm, and genuine, showing that the charm he exuded on stage was not just an act. This was the real deal, and it was refreshing to see.

After our time together, I received a text from Trump's team, inviting me to sit down for a one-on-one interview at Trump Tower. Talk about a surreal moment! As I walked through the grand entrance, I was met with the kind of security that would make Fort Knox look like a backyard BBQ. Secret Service agents were everywhere, and believe me, they weren't there to take selfies.

When I finally sat down with Trump, I noticed something unexpected: he was genuinely interested. We talked about everything from policy ideas to personal anecdotes. One moment that stood out was when he mentioned his efforts to hire a woman engineer to build Trump Tower at a time when female engineers were few and far between in New York. This was a man who believed in giving qualified people opportunities based on merit—not on gender or race. It was a refreshing perspective, and it made me realize he was much more than the caricature painted by the media.

We also discussed some ambitious plans he had, including the idea of having dinner together and organizing an event to honor the border patrol agents who had been wrongfully accused of misconduct during the previous administration. He was passionate about ensuring they received the recognition they deserved, and it was clear that he genuinely cared about the people who serve this country.

You see, the media often distorts the truth, spinning narratives that serve their agendas. But in that room, I saw a different side of Trump—one that was willing to engage and consider perspectives outside his own. "If you've got a good idea, I'm all ears," he said, and I couldn't help but respect that. It was an unexpected moment of candor that made me realize how important it is to break down barriers and have real conversations.

This experience with Trump made me reflect deeply on my own journey—both on the road performing live and in my conversations with everyday Americans. It inspired me to write this book, not merely to share my experiences but to emphasize the importance of talking to each other, of listening to one another's stories. In a time when division seems to reign, I believe it's more vital than ever to bridge those gaps through honest dialogue.

So, let's dive into the stories that shaped my path, the people I've met, and the lessons I've learned along the way. Ready to take a no-nonsense ride through the heart of America, where laughter meets reality and every conversation counts? Cool. Let's do this.

◆ 1 ◆

UNAPOLOGETICALLY ME

WHY DO LIBERALS HATE PEOPLE like me? They despise the fact that I refuse to fit into their neatly packaged identity politics. I'm a Black conservative, and I'm here to tell you that I don't need a political party to define me. I'm a free thinker, and that's what scares the shit out of the left.

And let's talk about that fear for a second. You see, the moment a Black person dares to step outside the confines of the liberal narrative, it sends shockwaves through the establishment. They don't just dislike Black conservatives; they loathe us. Why? Because we don't play the victim card. We don't wait for handouts or cry for help. We take ownership of our lives, our stories, and our futures. And if you think that's radical, well, welcome to the real world.

Let's rewind a bit. History shows us that Black Americans were once aligned with the Republican Party. Truth. After the Civil War, we recognized that the GOP was the party of emancipation. But somewhere along the line, the Democrats pulled a fast one. Shocker. They wrapped their arms around us with promises of civil rights and social programs, and we blindly followed. For decades, we were led to believe that the Democrats had our backs. Spoiler alert: they didn't. They merely saw us as political pawns in a game where they owned the chess board.

Fast-forward to today, and you'll find that the percentage of Black Americans identifying as Republican has plummeted. But a Pew Research study found that while 67 percent of Black Americans identified as Democrats in 2020, that number is declining. It's like watching a player slowly realize they've been dealt a bad hand. More and more of us are waking up to the fact that we don't have to be boxed in by the expectations of others. We can carve our own path, and that's where the real power lies.

Now, let's talk about the idea of victimhood. I fucking hate it. It's a debilitating mindset that keeps people chained to their circumstances instead of empowering them to rise above. I've seen it firsthand in our communities—people who refuse to believe they can change their lives because they've been conditioned to think they're victims. Shelby Steele hit the nail on the head when he said that the ideology of victimhood is dangerous. It stifles growth and perpetuates an endless cycle of dependency.

I grew up in a world where I was taught to believe in myself, to strive for excellence, and to take responsibility for my actions. My parents didn't raise me to look for handouts. They instilled in me the values of hard work, perseverance, and the belief that I could achieve anything I set my mind to. That's the message I want to send to every young Black person out there: stop waiting for someone to save you. You have the power to change your life.

The left can't handle that. They want us to remain in a perpetual state of needing their help, because that's how they maintain control. If we all started thinking for ourselves, it would be their worst nightmare. They'd lose their grip on the narrative, and God forbid we start to see ourselves as equals. That's why they attack us with such ferocity. They don't just want to silence us; they want to erase us.

But guess what? I'm not going anywhere. I refuse to be a pawn in anyone's game. I'm here to speak the truth, and if that means ruffling a few feathers, then so be it. I'll take on the left, the right, and anyone else who tries to stifle honest discourse. The moment we start censoring opinions is the moment we lose our freedom. And I'll be damned if I let that happen on my watch.

Let's talk about the so-called "Black leaders" who have sold us out for political gain. You know the names: Al Sharpton, Jesse Jackson, and others who have made a career out of being professional victims. They've turned pain into profit and have no desire to see real change. Why? Because if we actually succeeded, they'd be out of a job. It's a twisted game.

Meanwhile, the real heroes in our communities are the ones who are busy working hard, raising their families, and building businesses. They're not waiting for a savior; they're out there making things happen. And those are the stories that should be celebrated. It's time we shift the narrative from one of despair to one of empowerment.

Take a look at the Black conservatives who are making waves: Tim Scott, Allen West, and others who refuse to be silenced. They're proof that we can break the mold and redefine what it means to be a Black American. They're not just talking the talk; they're walking the walk. And that's what scares the left the most.

Let's also not forget our allies in the conservative movement. People like Condoleezza Rice and Colin Powell have paved the way for us, proving that we can hold high office and still stay true to our values. They've shown us that it's possible to love our country while advocating for change. The left wants to paint a picture of dissent, but the reality is that we can love America while holding it accountable. That's the beauty of being an American—we're allowed to critique and improve our country.

Now, let's shift gears and talk about the future. The tide is turning. More young Black Americans are starting to see the light. They're questioning the status quo and challenging the narrative they've been fed. Social media has become a powerful tool for change, allowing voices like mine to reach people who are ready to break free from the chains of political correctness. And I'm not just talking about conservatives; I'm talking about everyone—liberals, moderates, and independents who are tired of the divisive rhetoric.

The left can keep their echo chambers; I'll take the real conversations any day. I want to hear different perspectives, and I want to engage in honest discourse. The moment we stop listening to each other is the moment we start losing our humanity. We need to remember that we're all in this together, even if we don't always see eye to eye.

So, here's my call to action: let's embrace our individuality. Let's celebrate our unique experiences and perspectives. Let's challenge each other to think critically and engage in meaningful dialogue. And most importantly, let's reject the notion that we have to fit into any one narrative. We are more than the labels that society places on us. We are thinkers, doers, and change-makers.

It's time to rise up. It's time to take control of our narratives and rewrite the script. The left may want us to remain silent, but I'm not going to be quiet. I will continue to speak out, to challenge the status quo, and to empower others to do the same. We are not victims; we are victors. And as long as I have a voice, I will use it to speak the truth—no matter how uncomfortable it may be.

◆ 2 ◆

A WARNING TO REPUBLICANS:

CUT THE BULLSHIT WITH MICHELLE OBAMA

OKAY, AS TO THE RIDICULOUS political games being played right, now (happening as I write this book). If you think attacking Michelle Obama is clever, let me tell you—it's about as smart as throwing a boomerang while standing in front of a mirror. It's going to come back and hit you right in the face.

First off, let's address the absurd notion that Michelle Obama is going to run for president because a few knuckleheads on the right think they can make jokes about her being a man. Seriously? This isn't just silly; it's downright dangerous for the Republican Party. It's like we're playing poker with a deck stacked against us and deciding to go all-in on a bad hand. You think this is funny? I's not. It's a losing strategy that gives the mainstream media all the ammo they need to tear us apart.

Now, here's the deal: the Democrats have the numbers. We're always going to be outnumbered, so why would we hand them a gift-wrapped opportunity to mobilize their voters by attacking a woman—especially a Black woman? That's not just reckless; it's a recipe for disaster. Women of all backgrounds are going to rally behind her when they see their own being attacked, and you don't want to be standing on the wrong side of that battlefield.

Let's be honest about this. Every time someone out there calls Michelle Obama "Big Mike" or makes jokes about her looks, they're not just being disrespectful; they're shooting themselves in the foot. You think you're making a clever point? You're just adding more fuel to the fire. While you're busy trashing her, women across the country are rolling their eyes and thinking, "Really? This is how you're going to win us over?" Well, it's not working.

And remember that we just spent years fighting against the woke agenda. We've been battling for women's rights and equality, and then we turn around and make fun of another woman? You need to pick a side, people. You can't be the party that stands for women and then turn around and throw shade at Michelle Obama because you don't find her attractive. It's hypocritical, and we need consistency in our messaging.

I've seen this firsthand. Just the other day, I was out grabbing a bite to eat, and the waiter comes up and starts telling me a joke. He thought he was hilarious with his "Who Left the Seat Up?" joke about the Obamas. And I'm sitting there thinking, "Dude, you really think Michelle Obama is a man?" The guy was proud of himself, but he didn't realize he was just perpetuating a conspiracy theory that's as old as the hills. It's absurd! The first Black president was probably the most vetted man in history, and you think he would let something like that slip? Come on.

The Republican Party should be laser-focused on the future. We should be discussing the executive orders coming down the pipe, the work that needs to be done in our communities, and how to bring people together based on real issues. Instead, we're seeing news stories about how Michelle Obama looks, and that's just plain stupid! We need to be smart about our battles, not just loud.

Let's also take a moment to reflect on Trump's victory. It was a starting point—a fresh beginning that represented a shift toward common sense and hard work. I didn't just think Trump would win; I guaranteed that victory would be a slam dunk! And guess what? I was right! That's why you need to listen to me now. We've seen that a well-crafted message and a strong work ethic can resonate with voters. Throwing that away with ridiculous attacks on Michelle Obama would be foolish. We should aspire to that work ethic and common-sense approach, not dive headfirst into the kind of petty nonsense that turns voters off.

Remember, when Trump faced ridicule and mockery, he didn't crumble; he rose up and turned that energy into something powerful. We need to channel that same spirit. If we let ourselves get bogged down in childish insults, we risk losing the momentum we've built. We need to focus on the values that got us here: hard work, respect, and real solutions to the problems facing our country.

And remember the consequences of this nonsense. Remember when Trump was roasted by Obama at that dinner? That moment lit a fire under him, and he turned that mockery into motivation to run for president. You seriously think this current wave of attacks on Michelle Obama won't inspire her? You're kidding yourself! If she gets fired up and decides to run, we could be facing a formidable opponent. And I'm not sure our typical candidates—no offense to JD Vance or Vivek Ramaswamy—can match her charisma.

Let's also address the bigger picture. We're outnumbered, folks! The Democrats usually end up in the White House more often than we do, and that's not going to change anytime soon. So, we need to convince voters to cross over to our side. Starting off with, "Oh, by the way, your favorite president's wife is a man," isn't exactly the best way to win hearts and minds.

Look, I get that humor is part of politics, but let's use our heads here. How about we focus on policies, vision, and real arguments that matter instead of tearing each other down with petty insults? The left is more than happy to tear us apart, so let's not do their job for them. We have to self-police and hold our own accountable. If someone crosses the line, it's our duty to call them out.

This is a pivotal moment for us. The future of the party—and perhaps the nation—depends on how we handle ourselves right now. We can't afford to make fools of ourselves by engaging in petty attacks. We need to rise above the fray and show that we can be better than that.

So, cut the bullshit. Let's be the party of ideas, respect, and unity. Focus on what truly matters and leave the childish name-calling behind. Because if we don't, we might just find ourselves in a far worse position than we ever imagined. The stakes are high, and the clock is ticking. Let's play smart, not just loud, and show the world that we're better than this.

◆ 3 ◆

THE LOST ART OF LAUGHING AT OURSELVES

LET'S GET ONE THING STRAIGHT: humor is a delicate dance. It's a ride through the absurdities of life, and sometimes it takes a hard left into the uncomfortable territory. But those moments are often the ones that stick with us, that challenge us, and that, dare I say it, make us better. Yet, in the era of cancel culture and hypersensitivity, we're losing a vital part of our cultural conversation.

I mean, how sad is it that so much great art—comedy, specifically—wouldn't even make it past the first round of sensitivity training today? Picture this: Don Rickles, the king of insult comedy, would be run out of town faster than you can say "take a joke." The man made a career out of roasting people, and guess what? The people he roasted laughed right along with him. They understood the context. They got that it was all in good fun. But today? Nah, we'd rather take out the pitchforks and torches than appreciate the art of the roast.

Let's take a stroll down memory lane, shall we? Remember *Breakfast at Tiffany's*? Yeah, that's right. Mickey Rooney in yellowface as Mr. Yunioshi. Did it age well? Absolutely not. But was it a product of its time? You bet. And here's the thing: many people who watched it back in the day didn't see it as a call for cultural appropriation. They saw it as a comedy. Fast-forward to now, and that scene would be shamed, canceled, and probably pulled from every streaming service. What a loss!

And how about *Sixteen Candles*? Long Duk Dong was an over-the-top caricature of an Asian man, but you know what? A lot of people found it funny at the time. Today, that character would be the poster child for everything wrong with Hollywood. But let's be honest—if we can't laugh at ourselves, how are we ever going to grow? It's like trying to polish a turd—good luck with that!

Let's not forget *The Office*. A brilliant show that pushed boundaries, but also had its fair share of eyebrow-raising moments. Michael Scott makes jokes that are downright cringeworthy, but they serve a purpose—pointing out the absurdity of office culture and human interaction. The beauty of that show lies in its ability to make us chuckle at uncomfortable truths. Today, though? You'd be hard-pressed to find a single episode that could air without a disclaimer.

Oh, and what about Steve Martin dropping the N-word in *The Jerk*? It was a joke meant to highlight absurdity, not promote racism. The context matters—he was making a point about identity and how ridiculous labels can be. But today, that scene would be met with outrage, and Martin would be labeled a pariah. We're losing the ability to contextualize humor, and that's a damn shame.

Let's not pretend that comedy doesn't come with its rough edges. Life is tough, and comedy is tougher. As I'm out on the road doing my one-man show, I often find myself treading that fine line. Sometimes, I say things that might ruffle a few feathers. But guess what? You don't have to come to my show if you don't like it. You have the freedom to walk away, but why should anyone have the power to cancel my show because they didn't like a joke?

I've had to change venues more than once due to pressure over a remark I made about the LGBTQ community. Was I trying to be offensive? Hell no. I was trying to make a point, to make people think, and yes, to make them laugh. But in today's climate, the first instinct is to shut it down. We've created an environment where people are so afraid to speak up that we're stifling the very essence of comedy.

Let's talk about *Blazing Saddles*, a film that is the epitome of satirical comedy. It tackled race relations openly, using humor to expose the absurdity of racism. Today, would it ever get made? No way! It would be dissected, criticized, and ultimately buried under the weight of sensitivity. But that film opened doors for conversations that needed to happen. It made people uncomfortable, and that discomfort led to growth.

Now, I'm not saying we should glorify every offensive joke or stereotype that comes our way. But we have to recognize the intent behind the humor. Take *Friends*, for example. Sure, it had its issues with representation and gender roles, but it also captured the essence of friendship and the struggles of adulthood. Today, it's often scrutinized for its lack of diversity, but the show still resonated with millions. It made us laugh, and it made us feel seen.

Comedy is supposed to be a mirror held up to society, reflecting both the good and the bad. But when we start to cover that mirror, we lose something vital. We lose the ability to critique ourselves, to laugh at our flaws, and to find common ground through shared humor.

Think about it: if we can't laugh at our differences, how are we ever going to bridge the gaps that divide us? The beauty of comedy is that it allows us to explore topics that might be too sensitive for everyday conversation. It gives us the freedom to discuss the uncomfortable and the taboo while still finding a way to connect.

But in today's world, where every word is scrutinized and every joke is dissected, we're losing that freedom. We're becoming a culture that's afraid to laugh, afraid to be vulnerable, and afraid to tackle the hard topics. And that's a tragedy.

Let's face it: comedy is supposed to be rough around the edges. It's not always going to be pretty or easy to digest, and that's okay. Sometimes it's about making people squirm and think, even if it's uncomfortable. If we start to sanitize our humor, we're robbing ourselves of the opportunity to grow.

So, here's the deal: if you don't like my show, fine. You don't have to come. But let's not pretend that the world would be a better place if we canceled every comedian who dared to push the envelope. The beauty of comedy lies in its ability to challenge us, to make us think, and to show us that we're all in this together.

In the end, we have to ask ourselves: what kind of society do we want to be? One that laughs at its flaws and embraces its imperfections, or one that tiptoes around every potential offense? The choice is ours. But I know where I stand. I stand with the comedians who make us think, who make us laugh, and who remind us that it's okay to be human.

And if that means occasionally stepping on a few toes along the way, so be it. Because in the grand scheme of things, laughter is what connects us, and if we can't handle a few rough edges, we're in for a long, dull ride. So, let's embrace the comedy, the discomfort, and the beauty of laughing at ourselves. After all, life's too short to take everything so seriously.

◆ 4 ◆

LOOK WHO'S BACK (THE ALPHA)

GOOD NEWS. THE REELECTION OF President Trump signals the rise of a new kind of alpha male role model, one that can do a hell of a lot to improve our world. Now, before you start rolling your eyes, let's break this down.

First off, let's talk about what it means to be an alpha. We're not talking about some wannabe tough guy strutting around like he owns the place. No, a true alpha—like a good father—understands that peace often comes through strength. Think about it: a solid alpha male doesn't need to throw fists to command respect. He's got the ability to enforce boundaries and punish if necessary. That's what creates a culture of respect. When you've got a leader like Trump, it's peace by respect. The world leaders know who's in charge, and they respect that authority.

Historically, the role of the alpha male has evolved significantly. In primitive societies, the alpha male was often the strongest warrior, the one who could hunt and protect the tribe. He was the figure that commanded respect, not just through physical prowess but also through the ability to provide and ensure the safety of his people. Over time, as societies grew more complex, so did the definition of what it meant to be an alpha.

In the early twentieth century, the alpha male was often seen as the breadwinner—the man who worked long hours to provide for his family. He was the stoic figure, rarely showing vulnerability. But as the world changed, so did expectations. The 1960s and '70s introduced a new way of thinking. The traditional alpha began to be questioned. With movements advocating for equality and social justice, the landscape shifted. Men were encouraged to express their feelings, embrace vulnerability, and support their partners as equals. But somewhere along the way, many men felt lost.

The pendulum swung too far in some cases, and a new kind of narrative emerged—a narrative that often defined masculinity as toxic. Men were told that their instincts, their drive, and their assertiveness were problems to be fixed. This left many men confused about their roles, unsure of how to navigate the expectations of a society that seemed to be at odds with their very nature.

Enter President Trump. Love him or hate him, he embodies a return to a more traditional view of masculinity. He's unapologetic, confident, and he stands firm in his beliefs. He's built a reputation as a man of his word. While the propaganda machine works overtime to gaslight his accomplishments on the world stage, the truth is that world leaders know what's what. They recognize his strength, even if the left-wing media are hell-bent on undermining not just the president but the American way of life.

See, the alpha male doesn't shy away from confrontation. He faces challenges head-on. The world isn't always a friendly place, and those who think it is often end up as prey. When you have a strong leader at the helm, it sends a message that we're not going to tolerate the predators lurking in the shadows. You want to talk about child traffickers and pedophiles? They seek out the weak, the vulnerable—those kids without fathers present to protect them. It's a sick reality, and it's why we need strong men to step up and defend our families and communities.

Now, let's get one thing straight: President Trump is a good man, a fair man, and like all of us, he's flawed. I've met him, talked with him, and I can tell you he respected my family and me. And you know what? He didn't need a camera rolling to prove it. That's the true mark of a real person. Anyone can shake hands and make small talk in front of a camera. We've seen it all too often—some guy gives a homeless man a meal while filming himself doing it, all for the sake of virtue signaling. That's not genuine; that's exploitation of a poor bastard who's just trying to get by.

Trump wouldn't do that. He's not about the show; he's about substance. He understands that real respect comes from the heart, not from a scripted moment designed for social media likes. That's the difference between him and 90 percent of the politicians we see today.

What we need now is a revival of the alpha male who isn't afraid to stand for what's right. In a time when society often tells men to apologize for their masculinity, we need leaders who embody strength, resilience, and integrity. We need men who can model how to protect and provide without losing their sense of compassion and empathy.

So, what does this all mean for us as men? It means we need to step up and embrace the role of the protector, the provider, the alpha. We've got to lead by example, showing our families that strength is not just about physical power but about moral integrity and standing firm in our beliefs. It's about respecting others while demanding respect in return.

In a world where the lines are blurred and morals are often compromised, we need role models who exemplify what it means to be a true man. Trump's leadership style, for all its controversy, reminds us that sometimes you have to be blunt, unapologetic, and willing to stand your ground.

It's time to reclaim that alpha role, not just in politics but in our everyday lives. We need to teach our sons to be strong and compassionate, to understand that respect is earned, not given freely. We need to instill in them the values that will help them navigate a world filled with challenges and adversities.

So, let's embrace the strength, the courage, and the integrity that comes with it. Let's not just talk about making a difference; let's be the difference. Because when we stand as strong men, we create a safer, more respectful world for everyone. And remember, this isn't about being a bully or an oppressor. Being an alpha means knowing when to fight and when to walk away. It's about having the wisdom to understand that true strength lies not in domination but in the ability to uplift those around you.

In a society that often glorifies victimhood, we need to flip the script. We need to embrace accountability, not just for ourselves but for each other. That's how we build a community rooted in respect and strength. We need to stand together against the predators, whether they're in the form of societal challenges or personal struggles.

As we navigate this new landscape, let's encourage each other to be better. Let's foster an environment where men can be strong without being toxic, where they can protect without oppressing, and where they can lead without fear.

Let's be the leaders our families, communities, and country need. The future is ours to shape, so let's shape it with strength, integrity, and respect.

◆ 5 ◆

THE PULSE OF AMERICA

WHATEVER THE REASONS—WHETHER IT'S THE momentum of the success of the Greg Gutfeld show, the big moments I've had on Fox News, or the unbelievable success of my comedy tour—I've noticed something significant happening in the country. Looking at the polls a month before the election, I confidently called it a complete blowout for Donald Trump. There was no way anyone could look at Kamala Harris and f eel confident in her qualifications for office. I mean, let's be real: her speeches were uninspiring, and she was unqualified to be a district attorney, much less the vice president of the United States. The fact that she didn't invoke the Twenty-fifth Amendment to remove President Biden from office is mind-boggling. Whether she was complicit or a willing participant, the outcome is the same: both of them had failed the American people.

President Biden took an oath to uphold the office, and it's shocking that Kamala Harris hasn't faced more scrutiny for standing by while everything went to hell. She was supposed to break ties on major decisions, yet we had a president who essentially was a vegetable. The lack of action and accountability is infuriating. It feels like a betrayal, and many Americans are still struggling to come to terms with it.

The general feeling of panic, whether justified or not, has permeated our society. Good or bad, right or wrong, people felt uneasy about the previous election. COVID, mail-in voting, and a slew of other factors contributed to an overall sense of distrust.

What about conspiracy theories? If you had asked me a few years back whether there was a massive conspiracy to stuff ballot boxes, I would have laughed. "Hell no, that's ridiculous," I would have said. But after everything we've gone through in the last four years? Nothing would surprise me anymore. Think about it: Trump had the most Republican votes in history, yet somehow, seven million people didn't show up for what was touted as one of the most contested elections of all time. That alone raises eyebrows. When Trump won the previous election, it felt like a seismic shift in American politics, and now we're left wondering if we've been conned on a massive scale.

We were catfished as a nation. That's a fitting analogy. You know the feeling: you're talking to someone online who seems perfect, only to find out they don't exist. That's what it felt like. The media, the politicians—it all felt like a carefully orchestrated charade. The guy who was supposed to lead us was wandering off, mumbling incoherently, while someone else was pulling the strings behind the scenes. Meanwhile, people were losing their lives, not just in Afghanistan but in other tragic situations that we've been desensitized to. And there's this pervasive feeling that many haven't understood the gravity of what has transpired in our country.

Imagine feeling like you need a shower, but for some reason, you can't find the time. You're beyond musty; your clothes are sticking to you, and you're sweating profusely. Your hair is a clump, your beard is tangled, and dirt is under your nails. That's the kind of feeling many Americans have right now—a collective sense of grime and confusion. What's staggering is that no matter what corner of the country I found myself in—whether it was Oregon, Alabama, North Carolina, New Jersey, or Florida—every fan I met during my tour echoed the same sentiment: "I just don't feel good about the country."

A president symbolizes more than just a political figure; they're a point of pride and strength for many Americans. We want to believe we live in the best country in the world, that we're safe, and that our leader will protect us. But over the previous four years, nothing felt secure anymore. It was as if we were living in the story of "The Emperor's New Clothes"—our emperor not only lacked clothes but also seemed to lack the mental acuity required for the job.

During this chaotic period, I noticed that very few leaders spoke honestly to the American people. Very few acknowledged the collective anxiety and disappointment. I think I managed to do that. It wasn't a Republican or Democrat thing for me; it was a human thing. We have to fight for something greater than ourselves; we can't just lie back and accept the narrative that boys can play girls' sports, or that we should disregard basic principles of fairness and justice.

When every argument is met with accusations of racism or misogyny, it's a tactic designed to confuse and deflect. It's like being in a relationship where you catch your partner cheating, and when you confront them, they turn it around on you, saying you shouldn't have been snooping. You're left thinking, "Wait, you're the one who ruined our marriage, but somehow, I'm the bad guy for finding out the truth?" That's what the media have done to us. They've created a narrative that blames the American people for questioning their motives, and that's a crime in itself.

A lot of people were convinced by the lies. That's the biggest crime of all. It's not just those of us who called bullshit on the system; it's the millions who trusted these so-called experts and media personalities. Imagine if you were a diehard Trump supporter, hanging on his every word, only to find out that everything he said was a lie. You believed in him, marched for him, voted for him, and wore the red hats with pride. Then, suddenly, you're left feeling spit on and lied to. It would be a bitter pill to swallow.

So, what do you do when you've been tricked? You either keep going down the rabbit hole, because you're too stubborn to admit you were wrong, or you start questioning everything. Luckily, many people are beginning to question the status quo, and that's a beautiful thing.

I'm not talking about those talking heads on TV. If you want to learn about life and gain wisdom, you won't find it there. Most of those people are just reading from a teleprompter or regurgitating some talking points. They lack authenticity. That's why I cherish the moments I spend in the barbershop or at my kids' Little League games, or even in church, if that's your thing. Those are the places where real conversations happen—where we connect, laugh, share ideas, and talk about what's bothering us. The media have done a great job of getting Americans to stop talking to each other, and that's a shame. When we're not communicating, we're easily divided. The narrative becomes that if you don't agree with me, then you're wrong, or you're the enemy.

We've been split into two groups, and the twenty-four-hour news cycle has done its part to perpetuate the idea that the other side is out to destroy your way of life. It creates a toxic atmosphere that breeds distrust and animosity. Think about the good people who were lied to, bamboozled, hoodwinked—some even lost their life savings donating to the Democratic Party in the hope of fighting against what they believed was evil. This con job has left a trail of destruction, ruining relationships and families. We've become a society where people won't marry someone simply because of their political affiliation.

But when you get out there and start talking to people, the divide begins to close. You can break through the walls of prejudice with a simple, "Hey, how are you?" I've spent countless hours in meet-and-greets after my shows, listening to fans share their thoughts and experiences. It's fascinating. After the election, people came out in droves. They were no longer afraid to voice their opinions.

What's incredible is that my shows have evolved. They're not strictly political; they're about life, about the human experience. People from all backgrounds—Black, Hispanic, Asian, and everything in between—are coming together. It's a melting pot of stories and perspectives. And what everyone shares is a common feeling of unease about how things have been going.

Many of them believed in the vaccine, because that's what the news told them. They trusted the media, thinking they would be held accountable for their reporting. But then the media made a deal with one side to suppress the other. That's where the real betrayal lies. It's going to take years for our country to recover from this. People were hooked into a narrative that was far from the truth, and now they're trying to untangle themselves from those lies.

As a kid, I loved wrestling. I believed it was real, and for a long time, that's what I thought. Then one day, I discovered it was all scripted. That's a hard truth to swallow. Imagine living your entire life believing something, only to find out it was all made up. That's how many people feel right now. They've been misled, and it's hard to come to terms with that reality.

But here's the silver lining: people are starting to wake up. They're no longer pointing fingers; they're looking inward and asking themselves how they can be better. There's a collective realization that we need to work together, that we need to start paying attention to who we're voting for, and that we can't just vote for someone because their name sounds familiar.

I used to avoid talking politics with strangers. Now, when people engage me in conversation, I listen. I don't pretend to have all the answers, and I think that's essential. It's about understanding that we're all just trying to make it through life, trying to feed our families, and trying to pay as little tax as possible so we can enjoy our lives.

People are getting re-engaged in their communities. They're excited about the future. I've heard it everywhere I go: "It's going to be a great year!" People are optimistic, and that's contagious. It's not just isolated to one demographic; it's a sentiment shared across the board.

That's why I was so confident that President Trump would win the election. I saw it firsthand in the thousands of people I met across the country, people from all walks of life—young, old, gay, straight, Black, Asian, White. The message was clear: "We don't like the way things are, and we're ready for change." This isn't about political affiliation; it's about common sense.

We're reclaiming our right to feel safe in our country. It would be nice to reach a point where we can sleep at night with our doors unlocked. We shouldn't have to live behind six padlocks with a Rottweiler and a firearm to feel secure in our own homes. We're ready to get back to a place where we can trust our leaders and feel proud of our nation.

As I travel, I see the beauty of this country—the landscapes, the communities, and most importantly, the people. It's not just about the hotel rooms or the stages; it's about the connections I make and the stories I hear. I meet a sixty-eight-year-old Black man with tattoos, and we find common ground. That's what it's all about. Once you get past the surface, you start to see that we're all pretty similar.

People are ready to celebrate our differences without letting them divide us. The media want to keep the race card alive, but the rest of us are just trying to live our lives. When I meet fans after the shows, it's not about race or politics; it's about connection. They see me as someone they can relate to, someone they could have a beer with. That's what makes this journey worthwhile.

I'm always learning from the people I meet. Every conversation, every story shared, enriches my understanding of the world. It reminds me that while we may face challenges, the power of connection is undeniable. So, as I continue this journey, I encourage everyone to step out of their comfort zones. Engage with different people, hear their stories, and embrace the diverse tapestry that makes up this great nation.

in the end, we all want the same thing: to live our lives freely and with dignity. We have to face the bad actors, but we can't forget about the good people who are doing their best to make a difference. This country is beautiful, and it's filled with incredible individuals who deserve to be heard and respected. Let's keep the conversation going, break down the walls, and forge a better future together. That's what it means to be American.

So, if you have the chance to travel, do it. Meet the people, hear their stories, and celebrate our shared humanity. Because it's not about the color of our skin or our political beliefs; it's about the connections we make and the love we share. And that, my friends, is what will truly unite us as a nation.

◆ 6 ◆

THE DEEP FAKE OF THE BIDEN PRESIDENCY

REMEMBER IN THE LAST YEAR of Biden's presidency when Press Secretary Karine Jean-Pierre decided to take on the role of the truth police? It was a spectacle to behold, watching her stand at the podium, armed with her arsenal of buzzwords and deflections, ready to take on anyone who dared to question the integrity of her boss. This was during a time when videos of President Biden, showcasing his frailty and confusion, began to surface in alarming frequency, prompting critics to raise eyebrows and ask the tough questions about whether the president was fit for office.

Jean-Pierre, however, was having none of it. With a flick of her wrist and a roll of her eyes, she dismissed those videos as "cheap fakes." In her world, the term was wielded like a badge of honor, a way to deflect from the undeniable reality staring us all in the face. But let's take a moment to unpack this. What exactly did she mean by "cheap fakes"? According to experts, that means videos that have been edited to distort context and manipulate the narrative. Yet, isn't that exactly what her own administration was doing? In a stunning twist of irony, it was the Biden presidency that was the ultimate deep fake—an elaborate illusion crafted to distract from the chaos of reality.

The videos in question showed Biden in moments of vulnerability, appearing lost or unresponsive. In one particularly telling clip, he was seen being gently corralled back to a group of world leaders by Italian Prime Minister Giorgia Meloni after a skydiving demonstration. It wasn't an isolated incident; it was a pattern. We all watched as Biden seemed to wander off stage, talking to thin air, or getting lost in his thoughts while the world spun around him. Yet, according to Jean-Pierre, these were mere fabrications, the result of right-wing conspiracies aimed at tarnishing the president's reputation.

What was truly astonishing was the audacity with which she claimed these videos were altered or manipulated. "They are done in bad faith," she asserted, as though her own administration hadn't engaged in its fair share of spinning narratives and manipulating facts. It's a classic case of projection, where those in power deflect their own shortcomings onto their critics. The irony is thick enough to cut with a knife—the Biden presidency itself was a cheap fake, a carefully constructed façade that hides the disarray and incompetence lurking just beneath the surface.

As I travel across the country, meeting people at various events and gatherings, I can't help but notice a common thread in the conversations I have. Sure, there are jokes about Biden's condition—laughter about how out of touch he seems and how often he stumbles through speeches. But then, almost as if a switch flips, the mood shifts. The laughter fades, and a serious conversation ensues. It's not really a laughing matter. The reality sinks in: this is a man leading our nation who seems increasingly incapable of doing so. It's a sentiment echoed in towns and cities, from coast to coast. People understand that this is a very active issue—one that deserves attention and scrutiny.

Jean-Pierre's defense of Biden as a target of "cheap fakes" was more about preserving the illusion of a competent leader than addressing the real concerns being raised. It's a classic tactic employed by those in power: when the message gets too uncomfortable, twist it, manipulate it, and throw a smoke bomb to distract from the reality. But the truth is, it's not the videos that are the deep fakes; it's the manufactured narrative that the Biden administration has been peddling since day one.

Let's not forget the context in which these videos emerged. The Biden administration was gearing up for a presidential election, where the stakes were higher than ever. With Trump lurking in the shadows, eager to pounce on any sign of weakness, it was imperative for the White House to project strength and stability. But instead, we were treated to a series of gaffes and missteps that only served to raise more questions about Biden's capabilities. And when critics pointed out the obvious—when they highlighted the moments of confusion and frailty—the administration responded with a deflection strategy so absurd that it would make a circus clown proud.

What's even more baffling is the way the mainstream media played along with this charade. Instead of holding the administration accountable for its lack of transparency and honesty, they often fell in line, echoing the talking points fed to them. Jean-Pierre applauded certain outlets for "supporting" her claims, but what she really meant was that those outlets were willing to overlook the glaring inconsistencies and failures of the Biden presidency. It's been a disturbing trend that raises serious questions about journalistic integrity and the role of the media in a healthy democracy.

And remember the broader implications of this entire debacle. Trump won a second term in the hearts and minds of millions of Americans, and that speaks volumes. It's a clear indication that people saw through the smoke and mirrors, that they weren't buying the narrative being sold to them by Jean-Pierre and her cohorts. The reality is that many Americans had a front-row seat to the deep fake that was the Biden presidency. They recognized the incompetence, the confusion, and the outright lies that plagued his administration from day one.

But just because Trump won the 2024 election doesn't mean that the Biden administration and its staff should escape accountability for their actions. In fact, if anything, it's even more critical now that we hold them accountable for the chaos they unleashed upon the nation. The lies, the manipulation, the deliberate obfuscation of reality—these are not just political tactics; they are a betrayal of the American people. And it's one of the greatest scandals in presidential history.

Let's be real here: the culpability lies not just with the president but with the White House staff who orchestrated this entire charade. From the moment Biden took office, decisions were made that had monumental impacts on our country. But who was really making those decisions? Who was pulling the strings while the president was busy getting lost on stage? These are the questions that need to be answered, and the answers are long overdue.

We only know the tip of the iceberg when it comes to the true nature of this administration. The odds are very high that Biden was incapable of running the country from the very moment he took office, and we need to ask ourselves who carried on the business of governance during those times. The American people deserve to know who was really in charge. Who was making the calls on critical issues, like foreign policy or the economy, while the president was busy fumbling through speeches and forgetting key points?

The truth is, the Biden administration provided us a masterclass in deception, and now it's time for accountability. The American public has a right to know the reality behind the façade. It's not enough to move on from the catastrophic Biden presidency; we must pursue the truth and ensure that those responsible for the lies and the manipulation are held accountable. We must demand answers, seek out the facts, and expose the deep fake that has been masquerading as a legitimate presidency.

We owe it to ourselves and future generations to ensure that this kind of deceit doesn't happen again. The stakes are too high, and the consequences too severe. The American people deserve leaders who are honest, transparent, and willing to face the music, not those who hide behind a façade of false narratives. Let's peel back the layers of this deep fake and hold the Biden administration accountable for their actions. Because it's not just about politics; it's about the integrity of our democracy. And that's something worth fighting for.

As I continue to meet with people across the nation, I hear their concerns, their frustrations, and their hopes for a better future. These are not just jokes or passing remarks; they are serious calls for accountability. The laughter may come easily, but beneath it lies a collective understanding that we can't let this slide. We must be relentless in our pursuit of the truth, because only by confronting the reality of the Biden presidency can we hope to restore trust in our government and protect the values we hold dear.

People often say that they feel like they've been sold a bill of goods, and they're right. The Biden presidency was characterized by a series of broken promises and failed policies that left many Americans questioning the competence of their leaders. The rising cost of living, the border crisis, and the ongoing struggles in international relations are just a few of the issues that were neglected while the administration focused on spinning narratives instead of addressing the problems honestly.

The truth is that the Biden administration's approach to governance was anything but transparent. It spun a web of deceit that ensnared not only the president but also those around him. The staffers, the advisers, and the many figures behind the scenes all played a role in this orchestration of misinformation. They chose to protect their own interests rather than serve the American people. This is not just a political issue; it's an ethical one.

The American people deserve leaders who are willing to face the truth, no matter how uncomfortable it may be. They deserve accountability—not just for the gaffes and blunders, but for the systemic failures that have been allowed to fester under the guise of leadership. The notion that we should simply move on from the catastrophic Biden presidency is not only naive; it's dangerous. We cannot allow history to repeat itself. We must demand answers, and we must hold those in power accountable for their actions.

As we move forward, let's ensure that the lessons learned from the previous administration are not forgotten. The American people were not just passive observers in this story;

they were and remain active participants. They have the power to demand change and to insist on transparency. It's time to take that power seriously and to hold those in charge accountable for the deep fake that had been the Biden presidency.

Let's make sure we shine a light on the truth, even if it means confronting uncomfortable realities. Because ultimately, the integrity of our democracy depends on it. We owe it to ourselves, to future generations, and to the very principles that this nation was built upon. It's time to stand up, speak out, and demand accountability—because the stakes could not be higher.

◆ 7 ◆

WHITE LIBERAL PRIVILEGE

WHEN PEOPLE START TALKING ABOUT liberal White privilege, I can't help but roll my eyes. But let's take a moment to analyze it, shall we? And I want to give credit where it's due. Greg Gutfeld had a monologue that hit me like a freight train. He dropped some knowledge on the term "kayfabe." Now, for those who don't follow wrestling, it's the idea of keeping the business safe by protecting the secrets and illusions of the trade, and looking out for one another. It's a perfect metaphor for what the progressive left has been trying to pull off.

These folks think they're clever, using words like "kayfabe" to label President Trump a liar. But they completely miss the point. They try to paint him as the villainous manipulator of reality while they themselves are living in their own little bubble of fakery and hypocrisy. The truth is, they're the ones who play the game, spinning narratives to protect their own interests, all while claiming to be the champions of truth and justice.

Let's face it—debating these extreme leftists is like trying to reason with a brick wall. Common sense is on the right side of the aisle, folks. It's where to find the adult in the room, the voice of reason amid the chaos. You know what's represented in the Republican Party? Accountability. Transparency. Dignity. That's what we're fighting for. Meanwhile, you have the fringe left throwing around accusations like darts, claiming every White person is a racist, that there's this all-encompassing White privilege that somehow protects them all from the law.

I mean, let's consider White liberal privilege for a second. It's like a sick joke. You got a group of people who have no idea what it's like to live in the real world, and they're out here telling us White men have got it easy. They want to demonize White men for everything, from cultural appropriation to how we dress. A White guy wearing a basketball jersey? Oh my God, the horror! You'd think he was robbing a bank. News flash: I was a fan of the TV show *Vikings*, and they had long hair and braids, too. But somehow that doesn't count in their little narrative.

And please don't forget the absurdity of it all. You've got Tim Walz, that beauty of a politician from Minnesota, going after Elon Musk and Tesla while ignoring the fact that the company's stock is a significant part of his constituents' retirement plans. If Tesla tanks, it's not just a loss for Musk; it's a loss for thousands of Minnesota families. Yet, he celebrates the potential downfall of a company that fuels the livelihoods of the very people he's supposed to represent. That's a special brand of ignorance.

But it gets better. The people who are trying to turn public sentiment against Tesla owners are the same ones encouraging vandalism. Can you believe that? Keying a Tesla to "send a message" to Elon Musk? You're not hurting him; you're hurting the working-class people who can't afford to fix that damage. It's like shooting yourself in the foot and then wondering why you can't walk straight.

And then there's Tim Walz's assistant, who goes on a vandalism spree, gets arrested, and somehow doesn't face any real consequences. Why? Because, apparently, he can't lose his job if it means he can't pay restitution. Talk about a slap in the face to every honest citizen out there. If a regular guy pulled that stunt, he'd be behind bars faster than you can say "justice served." But because this guy is connected, he gets a pass. That, my friends, is White liberal privilege in action.

I mean, if I, as a Black man, committed a crime and used as my excuse that I needed to keep my job to pay the bills, do you really think that would fly in court? Hell no! I'd be treated like a criminal, no questions asked. But here we have a liberal White guy committing an act of vandalism, and suddenly, it's all about protecting his livelihood. It's a double standard, nothing but rank hypocrisy.

And don't even get me started on the "cultural appropriation" nonsense. You have people like the Walz assistant, who, while vandalizing a car, had the audacity to be wearing a Stephen Curry jersey. A Black man's jersey. So, let me get this straight: he's out there committing crimes while wearing the symbol of cultural pride, and that's not a problem? It's projection, pure and simple. They accuse others of doing the very things they are guilty of themselves.

It's a never-ending cycle of hypocrisy. They point fingers at us, claiming we're the problem, while they're the ones undermining our communities with their reckless behavior.

And the way they handle issues like transgender athletes in women's sports? It's absurd. We're talking about biological males competing against females in sports. It's not just unfair;

it's downright dangerous. This is not about inclusion; it's about common sense. When I was growing up, no one would ever think it was okay for a boy to shower with girls in a locker room. That's just basic decency. But now, we're supposed to pretend that it's all okay because someone decided they identify as a woman? No, thank you.

Let's be clear: this isn't about denying anyone their "identity." It's about protecting our daughters. It's about ensuring that the sanctity of women's sports is preserved. It's about acknowledging that there are biological differences that matter. We're not talking about hate; we're talking about safety and fairness.

And the people who push for these ridiculous policies are the very ones who turn a blind eye to the reality of what's happening. They ignore the voices of women who are being pushed aside in the name of political correctness. They're so wrapped up in their ideology that they're willing to sacrifice the safety and dignity of women for the sake of a narrative that isn't even based in reality.

So where does this all lead? It leads to a society where the lines are blurred, where common sense is tossed out the window, and where we're all left trying to navigate the chaos. And the truth is, it's exhausting.

I look around and see the absurdity of it all. I see politicians who are supposed to be leaders but are instead acting like children throwing tantrums. I see people who claim to care about justice while simultaneously engaging in the most hypocritical behavior imaginable. And I can't help but feel frustrated.

But then I remember that it's up to us to push back. It's up to us to call out the nonsense, to stand firm in our beliefs, and to fight for what's right. Because, at last, it's not just about me or you or any individual—it's about the future we want to create for our children, and the values we want to uphold.

We need to show the world that common sense and accountability matter. We need to hold our leaders accountable for their actions and demand better from them. Because if we don't, we're just going to continue down this slippery slope into chaos.

So, when I hear people talk about White privilege, I don't just nod along. I challenge them to look deeper. I ask them to consider the implications of their words and the reality of the world we live in. Because the truth is, it's not about race; it's about responsibility. It's about owning your actions and understanding the consequences they carry.

I've said it before, and I'll say it again. We're all in this together. We need to lift each other up, hold each other accountable, and strive for a better tomorrow. That's the only way we'll break this cycle and create a society that truly values fairness and equality. And that's a fight worth taking on.

◆ 8 ◆

THE DIAGNOSIS OF TRUMP DERANGEMENT SYNDROME

I NEVER THOUGHT I'D FIND myself in a position where I'd be discussing a medical condition, let alone one that has been labeled "Trump Derangement Syndrome" (TDS). But here we are. In a world where people are losing their minds over a former reality television star turned president, I think it's high time we diagnosed this phenomenon. And let me tell you, if the American Medical Association wants to hand out some fancy letters after my name for doing this, I'd be more than happy to accept the title of "Doctor of Common Sense."

Let's set the scene: you walk into a social gathering, and within minutes, the conversation turns to the one guy who seems to be more polarizing than pineapple on pizza. Whether you're at a barbecue, a wedding, or even a funeral, someone is bound to bring up Trump, and that's when you hear it—the unmistakable symptoms of TDS creeping in.

Symptoms of TDS: Please Be Aware

1. *Extreme Facial Contortions*: You know the look—the squinting eyes, the pursed lips, and that bizarre head shake that says, "Did you just say you voted for him?" When someone starts to sound like a character out of a horror movie, you know TDS has taken over. It's like watching someone try to swallow a lemon while debating with you the merits of The Wall.
2. *Outrageous Claims and Conspiracy Theories*: It starts off innocently enough: "Did you hear what he said?" But before you know it, the conversation spirals into a dark abyss of conspiracy theories about how he's actually an alien sent to destroy America. I mean, if we're going to go down that rabbit hole, let's at least make it fun. Maybe he's part of a secret society of reptilian overlords? At least that sounds more interesting than the actual news.
3. *Loss of Touch with Reality*: TDS seems to have an uncanny ability to warp people's perceptions. You've got people who can't go a day without bashing Trump, but when you ask them what policies they actually disagree with, they suddenly become the world's greatest experts on "feelings." It's like debating with a toddler who just learned the word "no." You can't reason with them; you can only nod and hope they calm down before they start throwing tantrums.
4. *Social Media Meltdowns*: You know it's bad when your friend's Facebook feed looks like a war zone. Every post is a barrage of memes, rants, and

hashtags that make you wonder if they've forgotten how to communicate without a keyboard. I mean, come on, Karen, you've got three kids—how about posting a picture of them instead of another angry rant about Trump's hair? At least it'll make your profile more interesting.

5. *Friendship Erosion*: It's amazing how TDS can turn lifelong friends into sworn enemies. You've got people unfriending each other over political differences faster than you can say "fake news." You'd think we were debating whether to put ketchup on hot dogs, not the future of the free world. But no, it's TDS in full effect. You may as well be discussing the merits of cannibalism.
6. *Job Losses*: I hate to say it, but TDS has serious consequences. I've heard stories of people losing their jobs because they couldn't keep their mouths shut about their political views. You know what? If you're working at a restaurant and you start yelling about how Trump is a fascist while serving cheeseburgers, you might want to rethink your career choices. You can't make a living by alienating your customers, buddy.
7. *Family Feuds*: Thanksgiving dinners have turned into battlegrounds, and heaven forbid you bring up politics. Grandma's mashed potatoes are now served with a side of passive-aggressive comments about "those people." Families are splitting over political affiliations like it's a new trend. I mean, come on, people! You can disagree without disowning your loved ones. Just agree to disagree,

and dive into that pumpkin pie, like we did in the good old days.

8. *Uncontrollable Eye-Rolling*: Have you ever seen someone during a political conversation roll their eyes so hard that you're convinced they might strain something? If you're witnessing this reaction, more often than not it's a telltale sign of TDS. Their eyes have become their weapon of choice, and it's a sight to behold.
9. *World-Ending Predictions*: TDS can lead to some wild predictions about the future. "If Trump gets elected again, the world will end!" they scream, as if he's the only person capable of starting World War III. Buddy, you might want to check your history books; there have been plenty of world leaders who could have filled that role.
10. *Compulsive Fact-Checking*: You know someone is deep in TDS territory when they can't have a conversation without pulling out their phone to fact-check every single statement. "Actually, that's not true. Let me Google that." It's like they're preparing for a debate with the president himself. News flash: you're not going to convince anyone by quoting a random Wikipedia page at a barbecue!

The Medical Implications

Now, let's get serious for a second. I'm not just throwing around terms for laughs here. TDS is causing real damage. People are losing jobs, friends, and family over their inability to engage in civilized discourse. It's an illness, and it should be treated as such.

Imagine a world where we could actually diagnose this condition. Picture the American Medical Association rolling out an official pamphlet: "Do You Suffer from TDS? Take Our Quiz!" They could include a checklist where you can mark off symptoms, like, "Check if you've lost friends due to political debates," or "Check if you've sent more than three angry tweets in a day." Honestly, we'd have a new epidemic on our hands.

The Path to Recovery

So, how do we treat TDS? First, we need to recognize it exists. Just like any other ailment, the first step to recovery is admitting you have a problem. If you find yourself spiraling into a state of rage every time you hear a Trump-related news story, it might be time to step back. Take a deep breath, look at the bigger picture, and remember that life goes on outside of social media.

Next, let's talk about exposure therapy. I'm not a doctor, but I can tell you that sometimes the best way to combat TDS is to engage with people who think differently. Attend a rally, join a debate club, or, heck, just grab a cup of coffee with someone who doesn't share your views. You'd be surprised at how much you can learn.

And finally, let's all just take a moment to laugh. Humor can disarm the harshest of opinions. If you can poke fun at your own side and see the ridiculousness on both ends, you're halfway to recovery. So, the next time you're at a family gathering and someone brings up politics, try cracking a joke instead of launching into a tirade. It might just save Thanksgiving.

At its root, TDS is a symptom of a larger problem: our inability to communicate and connect with each other as human beings. We've let politics seep into every corner of our lives, and it's driving a wedge between us. But if we can recognize TDS for what it is—a mental state fueled by anger, frustration, and a serious lack of perspective—maybe we can take steps toward healing.

So, here's my prescription: less outrage, more laughter, and a whole lot of compassion for our fellow human beings. And if we can find a way to laugh at the absurdity of it all, we might just make America great again—one laugh at a time.

◆ 9 ◆

THE LEFT'S SELF-DESTRUCTION:
THE TESLA TANGO

YOU KNOW, AS I TRAVEL around this great country doing my one-man show, I get to meet a lot of interesting folks. From the heart of Texas to the beaches of Southern California, the stories I hear are nothing short of enlightening. Just the other night, I met a guy in Southern California—let's call him Dave. Dave's a registered Democrat, a good dude who genuinely cares about the environment. A few years back, he bought himself a Tesla, not because he was some superfan of Elon Musk, but because he wanted to do his part to save the planet. You know, the whole "reduce your carbon footprint" spiel that was all the rage in the progressive circles.

Well, here we are today, and Dave is about as annoyed as a cat in a bathtub. He watches as his own party takes a sledgehammer to the ideals they once stood for, and it's infuriating. He can't believe that the very cars they once celebrated for their innovation and environmental benefits are now being targeted for destruction, simply because Musk decided to step outside the echo chamber of leftist ideologies. "What happened to logic?" he asked me, shaking his head. That, my friends, is the million-dollar question.

It's become a full-time job keeping track of this political soap opera, but here we go! The star of the show? None other than Elon Musk—once the golden boy of progressives, now cast as the villain in a farcical drama that's more absurd than a Three Stooges marathon.

Picture this: a few years back, Musk was the guy everyone wanted to have a beer with. The man was practically the poster child for the electric car revolution. He was saving the planet, one Tesla at a time, and progressives were throwing rose petals at his feet. "Oh, Elon, you genius!" they cooed, draping themselves in solar panels and dreaming of a greener future. But today, suddenly, he's the devil incarnate, the poster child for everything that's wrong with America. Why? Because he dared to associate with Donald Trump and push back against the government's suffocating grip on innovation.

This isn't just a disagreement over policies or ideologies. It's a full-blown tantrum, complete with protest signs that read "Down with Tesla!" and "Musk is a Menace!" Oh, the irony! These are the same people who once heralded Musk as a visionary. Now they want to burn his electric chariots in effigy? Talk about a plot twist worthy of a Hollywood blockbuster.

What's the meat of this madness? It's the hypocrisy that runs thicker than a New York accent in a downtown deli. The same environmentalists who championed electric vehicles and climate-change initiatives are now advocating the destruction of cars they once hailed as the future of sustainable transportation. Is this really where we are? Have we wandered so far that we're now sabotaging the very technology we once celebrated? It's baffling!

Let's break it down, shall we? The left has built an entire platform around the idea of saving the planet, and they found their hero in Elon Musk. He was innovating, creating jobs, and pushing the boundaries of technology. But then he dared to speak out against government overreach, and suddenly, he's a pariah. It's almost comical. The ones that once touted him as the second coming of Nikola Tesla now want to drag him through the mud because of his relationship with Trump and his controversial initiatives like DOGE.

Here's a thought: maybe, just maybe, the left should take a long, hard look in the mirror. Their response to Musk's actions is a perfect illustration of their extreme hypocrisy. They've allowed themselves to be consumed by a radical ideology that punishes anyone who doesn't toe the party line. And heads up; this isn't just about Musk. This is about control—control over thought, speech, and innovation.

And let's look at DOGE for a minute. This isn't just some meme currency; it's a symbol of defiance against a government that has, for too long, stifled creativity and entrepreneurship. Musk, with his cheeky tweets and bold moves, has managed to inject a dose of chaos into the staid world of finance. And for that, he must be punished! Who needs free markets when you can have a government-sanctioned monopoly on ideas?

But the left's radical approach is driving moderates and sensible voters away from their party. You want to know why Democrats are struggling in major elections? Look no further than this kind of insane extremism. They've painted themselves into a corner, alienating the very people they need to attract. The average American doesn't want to see their tax dollars going to smash Teslas in protest of a billionaire's political affiliations. They want jobs, security, and a government that works for them, not against them.

Remember when the left was all about unity? Yeah, me neither. Now, it's all about purging anyone who doesn't share their exact worldview. If you don't agree with every single aspect of their agenda, you're a target. It's a witch hunt, plain and simple. And in that frenzy, they're losing sight of what truly matters—the issues that impact everyday Americans.

Let's not mince words: this isn't just about Musk or Tesla. This is a symptom of a much larger problem within the Democratic Party. They've become so consumed by their ideology that they've lost touch with reality. They're fighting against the very innovations that could help make the world a better place, all in the name of a misguided sense of purity. It's a self-inflicted wound, and it's going to cost them dearly.

And here's where it gets really rich. The left loves to talk about privilege and power dynamics, yet they've created an environment where dissent is not just discouraged—it's actively punished. You can see it in how they respond to anyone who dares to challenge their narrative. They've turned into the very thing they claim to hate: an oppressive regime that silences opposition.

What's the endgame here? Do they really think that by attacking Musk and Tesla, they're going to win over the hearts and minds of the American people? Uhm... they're not. They're just digging themselves a deeper hole, one protest at a time. The more they lash out, the more they alienate the middle ground. And let's be real, the middle ground is where elections are won.

If the left keeps up this insane, self-destructive behavior, they might just find themselves on the losing end of every election for the foreseeable future. They're playing checkers while the rest of us are playing chess, and they're not even aware that the game has changed. They're stuck in a loop, perpetuating their own downfall, and it's a sight to behold.

In a world where innovation should be celebrated, the left is rallying against it, all because it doesn't fit their narrative. They've become the very thing they once opposed, and it's hilarious—if it weren't so tragic. The next time you see someone smashing a Tesla in the name of social justice, remember: it's not just about the car; it's about a belief system that's lost its way.

So, keep your eyes peeled. This isn't just a fight over electric cars and billionaires; it's a battle for the soul of a party that's completely lost. And as they spiral further into the abyss of extremism, the rest of us will be watching from the sidelines, popcorn in hand, waiting to see how this political drama unfolds.

◆ 10 ◆

WHAT TF IS HAPPENING TO LIBRARIANS?

BEING OUT ON THE ROAD, meeting people across America, it's like I'm getting a front-row seat to monitor the pulse of this country. Recently, I was doing a show up near Fresno, California, and after the gig, I held one of those meet-and-greet sessions. You know the drill: fans come up, share stories, and I get a feel for what's really going on in their lives. One couple stood out to me; they were heated about an issue at their local library. Apparently, the librarians were pushing some seriously graphic books right into the kids' section! Can you believe that? It made me think back to my own childhood and what librarians used to be like back in the day.

You see, when we were kids, librarians were these sweet, bookish types, right? They were our allies in the struggle against the horrors of school life. I remember trudging home from Mount Gleason Junior High School, a seventh grader with no friends within a two-mile radius. I moved around a lot as a kid—like, *a lot*. Rarely stuck in one place long enough to make a solid friend. But those library trips? Man, that was my sanctuary.

I'd stash some lunch money—because, let's be real, those Hostess Cream Pies were the real deal back then—and make a pit stop at the local grocery store. Once I had my sugary treasure, I'd hit up the library. I was on a mission: animal books, Godzilla, and whatever else sparked my imagination. Sure, I had dyslexia, so it took me a minute to sift through the index cards and sections, but when I found that book? Hell yeah! I'd check it out like I was on a top-secret mission. You'd fill out that little card, sign your name, and walk out like you just scored a championship trophy.

And the librarians? They were the best! You needed a book for a school project on dinosaurs? Boom! They had your back. It was like a self-serve buffet of knowledge. No one was judging you for wanting to read about wrestling magazines instead of math. The library was a haven where everyone was there for the same reason: to get lost in stories.

But then, something went sideways.

Suddenly, libraries morphed from magical realms of wonder into something else entirely. They became a playground for the homeless dudes who wanted to check out more than just books. And the smell? Oh man, it changed, too. It became less about the crisp pages of a new book, and more about something that felt off. The librarians? They changed too. It was like they went from helping you find the next great read, to pushing agendas.

You walked in expecting to see the latest books or the month's bestsellers, and what do you get? A rainbow parade of LGBTQ books and discussions about racism plastered all over the place. It's like you couldn't escape it. You'd roll your eyes, and the librarians were right there to tell you, "Hey, educate yourself!" What happened to the days of talking about

Charles Dickens? Now it's all about cutting your dick off. Seriously, what the hell?

It's like libraries turned into a cross between a political rally and a homeless shelter. They stopped being safe spaces for kids and became breeding grounds for confusion. This is where the invasion of our education system by radicals really kicked off. The last few years have seen our society crumble, and we're letting the worst of us dictate what's "normal."

Listen, I'm not a church guy, but there's something to be said about having some basic respect and morality in our lives. We're seeing kids get desensitized to everything. An eight-year-old shouldn't be reading about their first anal sex experience. What the hell? If your kid is gay or whatever, they don't need to be schooled on that stuff at that age. That's not how it should work.

We've stripped away the innocence of childhood, and it's a damn shame. When I was a kid, if you wanted to see something risqué, you had to work for it—like sneaking a peek at a *Playboy* magazine or catching a glimpse of something squiggly on TV. Now? Kids are bombarded with sexual content everywhere they turn. They don't understand boundaries, and it's all about instant gratification now, not about love or respect.

And you know what's even scarier? The lines have blurred so much that young men grow up thinking every girl should act like a Pornhub fantasy. That's just insane! When I was a kid, the idea was to treat women with respect, not as objects. But now, it's like we're raising a generation that thinks it's all about the latest trend, and that's destructive.

We need to take a hard look at what's happening. We're allowing a breakdown of morality, and it starts with our kids. If the first thing they see when they walk into a library is some sexually charged agenda, how can we expect them to grow up with any sense of right or wrong?

Parents need to step up and take their power back. It's not just about blaming schools; it's about being involved in our kids' lives. Social media is a minefield, and kids shouldn't have unrestricted access to it. It's not about being a helicopter parent; it's about protecting them from a world that's hell-bent on ruining their innocence.

Look, we've got to rebuild our communities, protect our kids, and stop letting the worst of us dictate what's "normal." We need to challenge the so-called educators who are pushing these radical ideas. It's time to expose the nonsense and demand accountability. Because if we don't, we're just letting the fabric of our society unravel, and that's a fight we can't afford to lose.

◆ 11 ◆

WHO REALLY RAN THE SHOW?

WHEN I HIT THE ROAD with my one-man show, one question keeps popping up from audiences across the country: "Who was really running the country during Joe Biden's presidency?" And you know what? It's a damn good question—one that deserves some serious air time. I mean, let's face it: if we're going to talk about the state of our nation, we need to address the elephant in the room. The guy in the Oval Office may have had his name on the door, but it sure as hell wasn't him making the calls.

I've been chatting with people from all walks of life, and the consensus is clear: we were being gaslit, plain and simple. You see, it's one thing for a president to have a few "oops" moments. We've seen that in the past. But it's another thing entirely when the leader of the free world is signing documents with an autopen while the country is crumbling around him. That's not just a red flag; it's a neon sign flashing, "Something's seriously wrong here!"

A recent analysis revealed that nearly every document Joe "signed" during his presidency was just a swipe of a fancy pen. The only exception? The one where he announced he wouldn't be running for re-election. I don't know about you, but that raises a hell of a lot of questions. What was he signing? Did he even know what he was signing? And who exactly was pulling the strings behind the scenes?

Let's be real here: other presidents have used autopens before, but none have shown the same symptoms of senility and cognitive decline. This is about a guy who, during his first days in office, was already struggling to string together coherent thoughts. House Speaker Mike Johnson put it bluntly when he pointed out that Biden signed an executive order mandating a pause on liquid natural gas exports without even understanding what it did. That's not just a mistake; that's a full-blown disaster waiting to happen.

So, who was actually deciding what got signed? Who was the mastermind behind the curtains, orchestrating the chaos that became the Biden administration? It's a mystery worthy of a prime-time thriller, and I'm here for it. The reality is, we may never know the full extent of the decision-making process that took place during those years.

Consider the flurry of left-pleasing executive orders that came pouring out of the White House in Biden's final weeks. It's like someone decided to throw a last-minute party, but the host was too out of it to even remember who was invited. How could a man who, months earlier, had revealed himself to be incapable of basic argument suddenly be churning out executive orders left and right? It doesn't add up.

Thanks to the utter lack of curiosity from our mainstream media, we're left in the dark about who was truly in charge. It's like they set up a wall of silence around the White House, shielding the inner workings from the American people, while we were left to fend for ourselves. The decisions being made during those years led to a string of disasters: an open border, rampant inflation, a catastrophic withdrawal from Afghanistan, and escalating chaos in global affairs. The Twenty-fifth Amendment didn't save us, and frankly, I'm not sure any law could have.

Now, let's address Congress for a second. This bunch of gerontocrats is supposed to be looking out for the nation, but they don't want to mandate regular mental health checks for our leaders. Instead, they let the president sign documents he probably didn't even read. If there's any silver lining in this mess, it's that we need to demand more. We should require that every president actually sign off on every law and executive order, not just slap their name on it. Give us some insurance that the person in charge is actually aware of what's happening in their own administration!

From what I've gathered, the decision-making process in Biden's White House was more like a game of telephone than a coordinated effort. Cabinet members weren't always communicating directly with the president. Instead, they were left to deal with his advisers—people like national security adviser Jake Sullivan and economic adviser Lael Brainard. It's no wonder that many cabinet officials felt their hands were tied. They were being fed information secondhand, and when they needed to raise an issue, they didn't always have to go through Biden. It was like playing a game of "who's on first" while the country was in freefall.

Take Agriculture Secretary Tom Vilsack, for example. He openly admitted that he had to explore multiple avenues to raise issues within the administration. What does that tell you? It tells me that the president wasn't the one calling the shots. It's as if they were all waiting for someone else to tell them what to do. The lack of direct communication with Biden was glaring, and it raises serious questions about who was truly in charge of the country's direction.

Even Janet Yellen, the Treasury Secretary, had to navigate these murky waters. She was kept at "arm's length," according to reports, and her interactions with Biden became more about dealing with his advisers than engaging with the president directly. And then there's Defense Secretary Lloyd Austin, who found that his access to Biden dwindled over time. Can you imagine that? The guy responsible for our national defense was struggling to get face time with the commander-in-chief. When your defense secretary can't get a meeting with the president, we've got a serious problem.

And recall how the Biden administration operated behind closed doors during campaign events. Donors were left shocked when they found out they wouldn't be getting a free-ranging Q&A session with the president. Instead, they had to submit questions ahead of time, and then they'd receive notecards with pre-approved questions to ask. Talk about a setup! It's like they were trying to keep Biden buttoned up, limiting his exposure to any real conversation.

What does all of this say about the state of leadership in this country? It says we need to demand better. We can't afford to have a situation where the president is merely a figurehead, signing off on orders without understanding what they mean. The ramifications of this kind of governance are mind-boggling. The chaos we experienced during Biden's time in office wasn't just a product of bad luck; it was a reflection of an administration that was clearly out of touch with reality.

So, what needs to happen now? First off, we need accountability. We need to know who was actually making the decisions that impacted our lives. Who was in that inner circle?

Who were the puppeteers pulling the strings while Biden was left in the dark? It's time to shine a light on the people who were really running the show. They need to be held accountable for the disasters that unfolded on their watch.

We also need Congress to step up and take a hard look at the processes that allowed this to happen. It's not enough just to point fingers; we need to implement changes that ensure this kind of situation doesn't happen again. Regular mental health checks for presidents? Yes, please! Mandating that they actually read and understand the documents they're signing? Absolutely! It's time to put some safeguards in place to protect the American people from being blindsided by inept leadership.

The question of who was really running the country during Biden's presidency is more than just a passing curiosity. It's a critical issue that goes to the heart of our democracy. We deserve to know who was making the decisions that affected our lives, and we deserve leaders who are capable of doing their jobs. If this experience has taught us anything, it's that we need to demand more from those in power.

So, as I continue my tour, I'll keep raising these questions, challenging the status quo, and holding our leaders accountable. Because in the end it's our country, and we deserve to know the truth. Let's not allow ourselves to be misled any longer. The American people are smarter than that, and we're ready to take back control. It's time to uncover the truth about who really ran the show during the Biden presidency—and make sure it never happens again.

◆ 12 ◆

THE LIBERAL CONDESCENSION COMPLEX

LIBERALS, BLESS THEIR HEARTS, LOVE to act like they've got the monopoly on intelligence. They swagger around with their noses in the air, convinced they're the only ones who truly understand the complexities of the universe, while they pat themselves on the back for their so-called enlightenment. It's like watching a toddler try to build a Lego tower while thinking they're constructing a skyscraper.

The left has this knack for treating conservative viewpoints like they're the intellectual equivalent of a participation trophy: "Oh, you poor little conservative! Did you come up with that idea all by yourself?" Meanwhile, they sit atop their ivory towers, sipping lattes and dismissing anyone who doesn't agree with them as ignorant or uninformed. This isn't just condescension; it's straight-up arrogance wrapped in a shiny bow of self-righteousness.

I get it. Every political group has its fair share of self-proclaimed geniuses who think they have all the answers. But when it comes to liberals, they've taken it to a whole new level. They genuinely believe that their views are not only correct, but also self-evident. It's as if they think they've cracked the code to human existence while the rest of us are still trying to find the instruction manual. And that's where the condescension kicks in. They look at conservatives as if we're wandering around in a fog, unable to see the light of reason and logic shining down from above.

Let me give you an example. Remember the whole healthcare debate? Liberals acted like they were the only ones with a grasp on reality, while they painted conservatives as a bunch of knuckle-dragging Neanderthals who couldn't possibly understand the complexities of health policy. When President Obama took to the airwaves and suggested that those who questioned the merits of his plan were simply misinformed, it was like watching a magician pull a rabbit out of a hat— while smirking in condescencion, as if he had knowledge of secrets that the ignorant rubes in his audience could never grasp.

Liberals love to claim that they're just trying to help us poor, misguided souls. But let me ask you this: when was the last time you saw a liberal genuinely engage with a conservative idea? I mean really engage—not just roll their eyes or dismiss it with a wave of their hand. It's like they're allergic to the possibility that someone with a different perspective might actually have a valid point. Instead, they'd rather hide in their echo chambers, where the only voices they hear are their own.

They've even got this cute little narrative they trot out: the "vast right-wing conspiracy." According to this playbook, conservatives aren't winning elections or policy debates because they have compelling ideas; no, it's because they're engaging in some sort of shadowy scheme orchestrated by puppet masters like Karl Rove and the Heritage Foundation. Forget that conservatives might actually have legitimate concerns about government overreach; in the liberal playbook, it's all just a clever ruse to distract from their own failures.

And then there's how they treat conservative voters. Liberals have this bizarre tendency to view anyone who votes Republican as a simpleton, easily manipulated by sinister forces. It's like they think average working-class Americans are so clueless that they can't possibly understand their own interests. "Oh, you're voting against your own economic interests!" they cry, as if we're all just pawns in some grand chess game, blissfully unaware of the pieces moving around us.

For instance, take Thomas Frank's book, *What's the Matter with Kansas?* Frank argues that working-class voters are so distracted by social issues like abortion that they're completely missing the bigger picture. It's like he's saying, "Listen, you poor, misguided souls! You should be voting for us because we know what's best for you." The condescension drips off the page, and it's infuriating. Hey, Thomas: people can care about multiple issues at once, you know. It's not either/or; it's both/and.

Then there's Obama's infamous "clinging to guns and religion" comment. Oh, that was a classic! He suggested that people in Rust Belt towns were resorting to their faith and their firearms because they were too dim to understand their own economic frustrations. Talk about a slap in the face! It's as if he believes that the only reason someone would cherish their Second Amendment rights is because they're too stupid to grasp the nuances of modern economics.

Here's the deal: people are complex. We don't fit into neat little boxes that liberals like to shove us into. They act as if we're all just a bunch of simple-minded folks clinging to outdated beliefs, instead of recognizing the layers of thought, experience, and emotion that shape our views. When you treat people like they don't have the capacity to think for themselves, you're not just being condescending; you're being insulting.

And then there's the way liberals love to frame conservative ideas as rooted in fear and anxiety. Al Gore, in his book *The Assault on Reason*, claims that right-wing politics are driven by a "gradual abandonment of concern for reason or evidence." Oh, please! That's rich coming from someone who insists on pushing climate policies based on fearmongering rather than solid science. It's a classic case of projecting your own shortcomings onto others.

While liberals are busy patting themselves on the back for their supposed intellectual superiority, they're missing out on valuable insights from the conservative perspective. The liberal narrative has, for far too long, stifled critical discussions about poverty, family structure, and the role of government. They've dismissed conservative critiques as mean-spirited or racist, instead of engaging with the valid concerns that underpin them.

Take the welfare debate, for instance. For decades, conservatives have raised red flags about the perils of long-term dependency. But instead of engaging with those arguments, liberals have preferred to vilify their proponents. They've ignored the voices of people who've experienced the pitfalls of welfare firsthand, opting instead for a narrative that paints all critics as heartless and uncaring.

It's time for a wake-up call. The deliberations over how to address poverty and its root causes need to be grounded in honest conversations, not knee-jerk reactions. If we're ever going to make real progress, we need to move beyond condescending attitudes and actually listen to each other.

But let's take a moment to appreciate the irony here. Liberals, who pride themselves on being open-minded and progressive, often resort to the same tactics they claim to despise. They'll rally against "bigotry" while simultaneously dismissing conservative viewpoints without a second thought. It's like they're playing a game of "do as I say, not as I do," and it's exhausting.

You know what else is exhausting? The endless parade of liberal celebrities who think their fame gives them a PhD in political science. You've got actors, musicians, and athletes weighing in on complex issues, as if their three-minute acceptance speech for some trophy qualifies them as experts. "Oh, I won an Oscar, so I must know what's best for the country!" Give me a break! Just because you can cry on cue doesn't mean you understand the nuances of economic policy or foreign relations.

And let's not pretend that these people are living in the real world. They've got their mansions and private jets, yet they're the ones lecturing the rest of us on income inequality. It's as if they think their bank accounts magically grant them insight into the struggles of everyday Americans. Meanwhile, they're sipping on organic kale smoothies while telling us we need to reduce our carbon footprints. How's that for hypocrisy?

Look, I'm all for people using their platforms to advocate for change, but when that advocacy is laced with condescension, it loses its effectiveness. If you want to connect with the average American, try speaking to them like equals instead of looking down your nose. You might be surprised at how far a little humility can go.

And speaking of humility, let's address the fact that liberals often act like they're the gatekeepers of morality. They love to throw around terms like "compassionate" and "progressive," as if those words alone validate their positions. But compassion isn't about labeling others as ignorant; it's about understanding different perspectives and working toward common ground. It's about recognizing that the world isn't as black and white as they'd like it to be.

But here's the reality: the liberal penchant for condescension doesn't just hurt conservatives; it hurts the entire political discourse. It stifles creativity, innovation, and constructive debate. When one side believes they have all the answers, they stop listening. And that's a dangerous place to be.

Let's also not forget the role of social media in this condescending culture. X (previously known as Twitter) and Facebook have turned political discourse into a battlefield where nuance goes to die. It's all about who can deliver the snappiest comeback or the most scathing critique, and the result is a never-ending cycle of outrage. Instead of fostering thoughtful discussions, we're left with a bunch of keyboard warriors throwing insults at each other like it's a game of dodgeball.

And here's a fun fact: studies have shown that social media can actually reinforce our biases. We end up following people who think like us, reading articles that confirm our beliefs, and blocking anyone who dares to challenge our views. So, while liberals are busy calling conservatives "uninformed," they're often wallowing in their own information silos, blissfully unaware of the irony.

But let's not let the liberals off the hook just yet. They love to paint conservatives as the party of "no," but let's be real: they can be just as resistant to change. When was the last time you heard a liberal openly admit that maybe, just maybe, a conservative idea might have merit?

And here's the crux of the matter: the more condescending liberals become, the more entrenched conservatives will be in their beliefs. You think calling someone stupid is going to change their mind? Please! All it does is reinforce their convictions. If you want to win hearts and minds, you need to engage with people, not belittle them.

So, here's my message to the liberals out there: your smugness isn't a substitute for substance. Your condescension won't win you any points in the court of public opinion. If you want to engage with conservatives, then do it with respect. We're not your ideological punching bags. We're not here for your amusement. We're here to have a conversation—one that includes all voices, not just the ones that echo your own beliefs.

Let's recognize that the path to progress lies in listening, understanding, and engaging with each other, regardless of our political affiliations. The future of our country depends on our ability to rise above condescension and build bridges, not walls. It's time to put away the labels, the superiority complexes, and the disdain. Let's roll up our sleeves and get to work—together. Because if we can't do that, then we're not just failing each other; we're failing the very ideals that make this country great. And I don't know about you, but I'm not ready to throw in the towel just yet.

◆ 13 ◆

ICE ICE BABIES

IMMIGRATION AND CUSTOMS ENFORCEMENT, OR ICE. Yeah, I said it. That four-word phrase that sends shivers down the spines of Democrats everywhere. It's time we took a hard look at what's really going on here, because the way Democrats are treating our ICE agents is not just a political issue—it's a matter of public safety, folks.

Let's start with the basics. ICE agents are tasked with keeping our borders secure, tracking down dangerous criminals, and making sure that those who come to this country respect our laws. But what do we see instead? A constant barrage of criticism, protests, and even legislation aimed at hampering their ability to do their jobs. It's like trying to play a game of football with one hand tied behind your back, while the other team is throwing rocks at you. How long are we going to put up with this nonsense?

Let's get one thing straight: ICE agents are not the villains in this story. They're not the stormtroopers of some dystopian regime; they're everyday men and women doing a job that is incredibly difficult and often dangerous. They put their lives on the line to track down individuals who pose a threat to our communities. I mean violent criminals, human traffickers, drug dealers—the kind of people who wouldn't think twice about causing harm to innocent families.

But Democrats have taken it upon themselves to paint these agents as the bad guys. Why? Because they're trying to score political points with their base. It's easier to rally the troops by vilifying law enforcement than it is to admit that, yeah, we need these people to keep our streets safe. It's a classic case of playing to emotions over facts, and it's putting lives at risk.

When Democrats defend illegal immigrants—many of whom have committed crimes—they're essentially standing in the way of justice. They're saying, "Hey, it's okay to break the law as long as you have a sob story." And let's be real: we all have stories. But that doesn't mean we get a free pass to break the law. It's called accountability, people, and it applies to everyone.

By defending lawbreakers, Democrats are sending a message that it's acceptable to disregard the legal process. They're compromising the safety of our communities and, more importantly, the safety of the very agents who are tasked with enforcing these laws. What kind of message does that send to our ICE agents? "You're on your own out there; good luck dealing with the consequences of our political games." It's downright shameful.

Let's consider the safety of our ICE agents for a moment. These folks are out there every day, sometimes in dangerous neighborhoods, trying to apprehend individuals who may not be too keen on being apprehended. Imagine being an ICE agent and going into a situation where you know that the person you're dealing with has a history of violence. Now, imagine knowing that your own government is doing everything in its power to undermine your ability to do that job safely. It's like being a firefighter who's been told to put out a fire, but isn't allowed to bring a hose.

What happens when ICE agents are forced to operate in a hostile environment? They become targets. I've seen reports of agents being harassed, threatened, and even physically attacked while trying to do their jobs. And why? Because they're seen as the enemy by those who ought to be supporting them. It's a toxic environment, and it's only going to get worse if we keep allowing politicians to play these games.

Now, let's recall the political theater surrounding ICE. You've got politicians standing in front of cameras, clutching their pearls, and talking about family separations and humanitarian crises. Sure, those are important issues, but let's not act like the people working for ICE are heartless monsters. They're trying to do their jobs in a system that is fraught with challenges. And many of them are trying to strike a balance between enforcing the law and being compassionate. It's not as simple as "lock them up and throw away the key." But you wouldn't know that from the way it's portrayed in the media.

Instead of working toward solutions, politicians are more interested in stoking outrage. They want to show their base that they're "fighting the good fight" against the so-called "ICE monsters." But in reality, they're just making it harder for these agents to do their jobs effectively. The more they demonize ICE, the more they put the lives of these agents—and the citizens they're trying to protect—at risk.

Let's next take a moment to acknowledge the human element here. ICE agents are not just numbers on a spreadsheet; they're parents, brothers, sisters, and friends. They have lives outside of their jobs, and they're just trying to make a living while keeping our communities safe. And when they're constantly under attack, it takes a toll. It's not just about the physical danger; it's about the mental and emotional strain as well.

I can only imagine the stress these agents face when they go home after a long day. They're tasked with making decisions that could impact lives, and then they have to deal with the fallout from politicians who are more interested in scoring points than in supporting law enforcement. What kind of pressure does that put on them? It's a heavy burden to bear, and it's time we acknowledged that.

So, what's the solution? First and foremost, we need to stop treating ICE agents like the enemy. They're our allies in the fight against crime and illegal immigration. Instead of condemning them, we should be supporting them. We need to allow them to do their jobs without the constant fear of political repercussions. If we want to have a rational conversation about immigration, we need to acknowledge that law enforcement plays a vital role in that discussion.

Secondly, Democrats need to stop defending lawbreakers at the expense of public safety. It's time to recognize that there are consequences for breaking the law, no matter how compelling the backstory might be. Compassion is important, but it shouldn't come at the cost of safety and security. We can't ignore the fact that some individuals pose a genuine threat to our communities, and we can't allow politics to cloud our judgment on this issue.

We also need to encourage dialogue. It's time for politicians to sit down with ICE agents and have an honest conversation about the challenges they face. They should be working together to find solutions, not playing political games that put lives at risk. It's time to move past the sensationalism and focus on what really matters: keeping our communities safe.

This isn't just about politics; it's about people. It's about the families who depend on ICE agents to keep them safe and the agents themselves who are risking everything to do their jobs. We need to remember that when we're having these discussions.

Let's put an end to the demonization of ICE and recognize the important role they play in protecting our communities. Let's support them instead of undermining them. Because if we don't, we're not just failing our law enforcement; we're failing ourselves. And quite frankly, that's not a situation we can afford to be in.

◆ 14 ◆

THE CASE FOR ELDER ABUSE

OKAY, LET'S GET REAL. WE'RE living in a world where leaders are supposed to be the best and brightest among us. Yet there we were, watching a man who should have stepped aside long ago still trying to hold on to power. And the one person who had been right there with him, pushing him to run again, was none other than Jill Biden. I'm not here to throw shade on her as a person, but let's break down why she should be facing elder abuse charges for her role in this whole mess.

First off, let's clarify what elder abuse actually is. According to the National Center on Elder Abuse, it includes a range of actions that harm or put at risk the well-being of an older adult. This can be physical abuse, emotional abuse, financial exploitation, neglect, and yes—psychological manipulation. When we talk about elder abuse in the context of someone like Joe Biden, we're looking at the psychological aspect. This is about ensuring that someone who is vulnerable—due to age or health—has their best interests protected.

Now, let's break it down even further. Imagine your loved one is in a state of mental decline. Are you really going to push them to do something as high-pressure and demanding as running for president? That's not just questionable; it's downright irresponsible. It's like watching someone who can barely walk trying to climb Mount Everest. You don't cheer them on; you step in and say, "Hey, maybe it's time to reconsider."

We're not talking about some vague assumptions here. Jill Biden was well aware of her husband's health issues—his cognitive decline, his cancer diagnosis, the whole nine yards. Reports have shown that he had aggressive prostate cancer that had spread to his bones. And still, she was out there, front and center, encouraging him to run for a second term. That's not just enabling; that's a blatant disregard for the well-being of an elder who is clearly not fit for the job.

Let's not forget the debates. During those televised smackdowns, Joe Biden was visibly struggling. He stumbled over words, lost his train of thought, and exhibited classic signs of cognitive decline. Did Jill Biden step in to protect him from public humiliation? No. Instead, she continued to support his candidacy. If that doesn't scream elder abuse, I don't know what does.

Now, here's where it gets even murkier. There's an ethical obligation for anyone in a position of power to be transparent about their health, especially when it comes to running for the highest office in the land. By keeping Joe's health issues under wraps, Jill Biden wasn't just shielding him; she was misleading the public. Americans deserve to know the truth about the health of their leaders. It's not just about the individual; it's about the integrity of the office.

When you're in the public eye, your health is part of the deal. If you're not fit to serve, then you shouldn't be serving. Period. By pushing Joe to run, Jill Biden was not only ignoring the signs but also failing the American people. It's hard to argue that this isn't elder abuse when you consider the implications of such a cover-up.

Now, some might say, "But Tyrus, this is a personal matter! Why should she face charges?" Well, there's a difference between ethical responsibility and legal responsibility. While Jill may not have physically harmed Joe, the psychological ramifications of her actions can be just as damaging. If you're enabling someone to make decisions that are clearly harmful to them, especially when they cannot fully comprehend those decisions, you're crossing a line.

Imagine a scenario where a family member with dementia is pushed to sign over their assets or make big life decisions. That's not just unethical; it's illegal. So why are we holding Jill Biden to a different standard? Just because she's in the public eye? That's nonsense.

Let's also consider the cognitive decline aspect. Joe Biden's public appearances were marked by confusion and forgetfulness. He couldn't remember details, mixed up facts, and had moments where he seemed completely lost. This isn't just a sign of aging; it's a serious health issue. When someone is in that state, they aren't able to make informed decisions. They're vulnerable, and that vulnerability should be protected, not exploited for political gain.

Jill Biden's actions can be seen as a form of exploitation. By encouraging Joe to run for office and allowing him to campaign, she was essentially putting her ambitions above his health. That's not love; that's manipulation. Elder abuse isn't always about physical harm; sometimes it's about emotional and psychological exploitation, and that's exactly what this situation illustrates.

Now let's consider the fallout from this whole situation. The public trust has been eroded, and the reputation of the Biden family has taken a serious hit. When you have people like Leo Terrell from the Department of Justice suggesting that charges should be brought against Jill, you know the stakes are high. This isn't just about one family; this is about the integrity of leadership in this country. If we allow this kind of behavior to slide, what message does that send?

It says that it's okay to ignore the needs of the vulnerable if it serves somebody's self-serving idea of a "higher" agenda. It tells other families in similar situations that they can do the same. And that, my friends, is a slippery slope.

So, what should happen next? If we want to uphold some semblance of accountability in our political system, we have to start with the people who are in it. Jill Biden should be held accountable for her actions—or lack thereof. It's time to take a stand against elder abuse in all its forms, whether it's in a nursing home or the White House.

The truth is, we need to start having real conversations about the health of our leaders. Transparency should be the standard, not the exception. If someone isn't fit for office, they shouldn't be running. It's that simple. And if their loved ones are pushing them to do so, we need to call that out for what it is: elder abuse.

This isn't just about Jill Biden; it's about the future of our political landscape. It's about ensuring that the leaders we elect are capable and ready to serve. We owe it to ourselves and to future generations to make sure that elder abuse—whether in the form of manipulation, exploitation, or neglect—has no place in our government.

America deserves better, and it's time to demand it. So, let's start holding those in power accountable, because if we don't, we're just as complicit in the abuse. It's time to stand up, speak out, and make sure that our leaders are not only fit to serve but also respected and cared for in their golden years.

◆ 15 ◆

THE HUSTLE OF BELIEF

I'VE DONE SOME STUDYING ON the Mormon Church, and honestly, that's probably the funniest religion for me. You can literally see the hustle from a mile away. Now, don't get it twisted—I'm not here to knock anyone's beliefs. I think everyone has the right to believe what they want. My issue isn't with faith itself; it's when people start pushing their beliefs onto others. We've got enough going on in this country without adding a religious debate to the pile.

When I say we could all use a little religion, I mean it in a broader sense. We need to get back to some basic moral principles—be good to your neighbor, honor your wife, honor your husband, and just treat people with respect. There used to be a time when men dressed up for success. You'd see them in suits and hats, walking out the door like they meant business. Now, I'm a guy who wears sweats on TV—my favorite sweats, mind you, which are hip-hop-inspired and part of my brand. But even I know when to put on a suit. What I'm talking about is basic decency in how we present ourselves.

You don't need to walk around with your butt hanging out of your pants or show off your areolas to make a statement. I get it—people have the right to dress how they want; but there are reasons we have societal norms. A lot of those norms were put in place because men have a penchant for wickedness, particularly when it comes to women. We used to have rules that kept things in check, and now it feels like we've tossed them out the window.

It's not about being conservative or traditional; it's about common sense. When you present yourself in a certain way, it can discourage unwanted attention. I'm not saying that evil people won't do evil things; they will. But let's face it, dressing modestly can help reduce the number of unwanted advances. It's about self-respect and how you carry yourself.

You know, I think a lot of the issues we see today come from a breakdown of that moral code. People are out here selling their bodies for clicks and likes, and I can't help but wonder: is this really what we want? Influencers are flaunting themselves online, and it's become a race for attention. Women are putting themselves out there in ways that make you question who's filming them. More often than not, it's their husbands or boyfriends, and I think, "Is this really the best way to make a living?"

We need to find better ways to express ourselves. Sure, we all go through dark times, but we shouldn't be glorifying this lack of morals. And let's talk about education for a second. I think we should start every school day with the Pledge of Allegiance. It sets the tone for what you're there for: to be a part of something bigger, to work towards the American dream of owning a home, having a family, and enjoying the fruits of your labor.

We need to teach kids that being in school is about more than just showing up; it's about responsibility and community.

Yet, when I hear atheists on TV going off about their (lack of) beliefs, I can't help but smirk because they're still following the rules that come from those very same traditional moral codes. You can say you don't believe in God, but if you're still abiding by the laws that those teachings laid down, aren't you just practicing religion in a different form?

I think that's where the confusion lies. You've got idiots out here virtue signaling, acting like they're above it all, but they're still living by the same rules. It's almost arrogant, like they're mocking those who do believe. If someone's devoutly religious, whether they're Muslim, Buddhist, or whatever, I think we should respect that. But they should also respect those who don't share their beliefs.

I made a deal with myself: If there is a God, I'm going to follow the rules that are in place, but I'm not going to church. Instead, I want to make my own choices, and I don't need anyone telling me how to live my life. It's not that I have a problem with people who go to church; I think it's important for many. But we need to get back to a simple, commonsense moral code in this country.

And I think it's starting to happen. Look, 50 percent of the internet is used for pornography, which means young men are watching unrealistic portrayals of women. It's not just affecting their expectations; it's creating a hyper-sexualized culture where women feel pressured to compete for attention. The so-called influencers are out there asking, "Would you date me?" while posing in ways that would make you question their own self-worth.

Did anyone ever stop and think about who's filming these women? Often, it's their partners, and that should raise some red flags. It's a vicious cycle, and I just can't help but think there are better ways to navigate life than selling pictures of your body. We need to instill a sense of self-respect and establish a moral code that goes beyond likes and follows.

I've always said boys and girls are different, and they need to be raised differently. Boys need discipline and an outlet for their energy. They shouldn't be sitting in church for two hours, staring at the ceiling. They need to be outside, climbing trees, getting scrapes and bruises. That's how you build men. They need to know what accountability is, what the laws are, and how to treat others.

We've replaced the Bible with the tablet, and the craving for instant gratification has warped our social structure. If I can't win a game, I'll just buy my way to victory. That's not how life works. People used to have a sense of community; if someone cut you off in traffic, you'd yell, "Hey, watch out!" Now, people are following each other home and escalating things to violence. It's a misplaced rage that stems from not getting what we want when we want it.

I'm proud to say I've never spent a night behind bars. No matter where I was in my life, I had a strong sense of accountability. I might've gotten away with some things, but I respected the rules. If someone wanted to infringe on my freedom, I had no problem stepping back and saying, "No, thank you."

I wasn't religious, but I educated myself about it. I wanted to understand what people were talking about when they mentioned that sparkle or tingle they get from faith. It just wasn't there for me. But that doesn't mean I don't respect the teachings that have been handed down through generations.

Organized religion, especially Christianity, has served our country well. When it's applied correctly, it benefits us all. And

I think we need to be able to speak on that. If someone wants to pray before starting their day, they should be able to do that without fear of judgment. It shouldn't just be about one group getting a seat at the table while others are pushed aside.

I've always had an issue with micromanaging and grouping people, especially regarding religion. We all need to be better at respecting one another's beliefs. Just because someone doesn't believe the way you do doesn't mean they're not following the same basic principles. It's all about interpretation, and I think we often manipulate it to fit our needs.

Take the commandment "Thou shalt not kill." It's a straightforward rule, but somehow it gets twisted. People use religion to justify actions that go against those very teachings. That's why I'm skeptical of organized religion; it often feels like it serves those in power rather than advancing the actual message.

When I see preachers in $5,000 suits while families struggle to make ends meet, I have to question their system. Why is it that the guys preaching to us seem to be living high on the hog while their congregation is struggling? It doesn't sit right with me, and that's why I've distanced myself from organized religion. It's flawed because it's run by people, and people will always bend the rules to fit their agendas.

That said, we need to separate our beliefs from the general good messages that come from the Bible: law and order, love and support for your neighbors, and being a decent person. We're losing sight of that in this society, and it's time to get back to basics.

If we could all start respecting each other's beliefs while focusing on the commonalities that unite us, we'd be in a much better place. We should remember that we're all trying to navigate the same life problems, and we need to do it with a sense of community and shared values.

We need those teachings now more than ever to turn around what has been four years of absolute lunacy. So, let's get back to a moral code that means something, and let's do it together. That's how we can build a better future for everyone.

◆ 16 ◆

TIME TO CUT THE CHECK

THE FEDERAL GOVERNMENT JUST PULLED over $2.2 billion in grants and $60 million in contracts from Harvard University because they decided to throw a tantrum and defy the Trump administration. And you know what? Good! It's about time we stop the funding merry-go-round for these elite institutions that have become little more than breeding grounds for radical ideologies and social-media-infused ignorance.

Harvard, with its shiny $50 billion-plus endowment, wants to act like a petulant child, throwing a fit because they can't get their way. They're saying they won't comply with the government's demands to limit activism on campus. And what kind of activism are we talking about? We're not talking about Martin Luther King Jr. marching for civil rights; we're talking a bunch of spoiled, privileged, wet-behind-the-ears students, who abandon their classrooms to "save the world" by raising hell through destructive and threatening acts.

You ever wonder why we're shoveling billions of taxpayer dollars into these institutions? I mean, seriously, what are we getting in return? A bunch of graduates who can't even find their way out of an X thread without getting lost? These universities claim to be the bastions of knowledge and enlightenment, yet they produce thousands—no, millions—of young people who have no clue about the real world.

Let's take a stroll down memory lane, shall we? Harvard, Yale, Princeton—they all have storied histories, but what have they produced recently? A generation of students who can't even agree on what a woman is, yet they're more than happy to tell you how to run your life. They've turned education into a political battleground, where dissenting opinions are met with outrage instead of debate.

These schools have become conformity camps, where only one ideology is allowed to thrive: the radical leftist agenda. And the result? A bunch of graduates who think they're the gatekeepers of morality, yet who are completely clueless about the realities of everyday life. They've spent four years inside an opinion bubble, and now they're stepping into the world with a skewed perspective that's dangerously out of touch.

These Ivy League schools have turned into indoctrination stations, where radical professors preach their gospel to unsuspecting students. You think you're sending your kid to learn about economics? Nah, they're getting a crash course in Marxism, instead. And how about the so-called "diversity" initiatives. It's like they've taken the word and twisted it into a pretzel, serving up a brand of "inclusivity" that *excludes* anyone who disagrees with their narrow-minded worldview.

Take a look at the curriculum. What used to be a robust education in critical thinking has now morphed into a checklist of leftist ideologies. Students are taught to shout down dissenters instead of engaging in civil discourse. If you don't believe me, just look at the countless videos of college students protesting speakers who dare to challenge their beliefs. They're not there to learn; they're there to enforce conformity.

And let's address antisemitism, shall we? These institutions want to fight it? Great! Start by cleaning house. You can't claim to stand against hate while simultaneously fostering a culture that allows it to flourish. If they want to keep their funding, they better start aligning their actions with their words. Otherwise, why should we, the taxpayers, keep funding their hypocrisy?

Let's face it: the elite have gotten comfortable. They've been living in their ivory towers for too long, sipping on their overpriced lattes while the rest of us are out here hustling to make ends meet. Harvard graduates are stepping into powerful positions, and what do they do? They push policies that further divide us, while claiming to be the champions of peace and equality.

You want to talk about privilege? How about the privilege of getting a degree from an institution like Harvard, only to come out with a worldview that's completely disconnected from reality? If you're a middle-class American working two jobs just to keep your head above water, you're not seeing the benefits of that elite education. Instead, you're watching helplessly as these graduates implement policies that hurt your community—all in the name of "progress."

And remember the irony here. These schools preach about equality and social justice, yet they charge astronomical tuition fees that only the wealthiest can afford. They're perpetuating a cycle of privilege while masquerading as champions of the underprivileged. If they truly cared about social equity, they'd be doing more to lower their tuition costs and make education accessible to all. But instead, they're happy to rake in the cash while telling everyone how to live their lives.

Now, some people will argue that cutting off funding to these institutions is a slippery slope. They'll tell you that without federal dollars, tuition will skyrocket, and only the rich will be able to attend. Well, here's a little secret: tuition is already skyrocketing, and it's not because of a lack of funding. It's because these schools know they can get away with charging ridiculous amounts because they've created a system that values prestige over practicality—subsidized by the taxpayers. Federal support allows them to expand their staffs and pad their salaries...which raises the costs. It's a never-ending cycle.

Let's be clear: the idea that these elite institutions are the only path to success is a myth. There are countless alternatives out there—community colleges, trade schools, online courses—that provide valuable education without the astronomical price tag. If Harvard and its Ivy League buddies are as great as they claim to be, they'll survive without our taxpayer dollars. They'll find other ways to fund their programs, whether through private donations or alumni contributions. But if they can't sustain themselves without federal funding, maybe it's time to reevaluate their worth.

Let's dive deeper into the hypocrisy of these institutions. Harvard and other elite schools love to tout their commitment to diversity, but what does that really mean? It often translates to a superficial commitment to racial and gender quotas while ignoring the *diversity of thought*. If you don't fit their mold, you're out. This isn't about true diversity; it's about creating a façade that makes them look good on paper.

And the real world isn't just about identity politics. It's messy, complex, and requires the ability to think critically and engage with opposing viewpoints. But these universities have chosen to stifle that kind of dialogue in favor of a "safe-space" mentality, which shields students from viewpoint challenges. They're teaching students to be sensitive, but not resilient, and that's a dangerous lesson to learn.

Imagine walking into a boardroom filled with people who all think the same way. What kind of innovative ideas are going to come from that? None, of course. The world needs thinkers who can challenge the status quo, not a bunch of yes-men who are afraid to voice their opinions for fear of being "canceled."

Let's consider the real issue here: the burden on taxpayers. Why are we, the hard-working citizens of this country, subsidizing institutions that have lost their way? It's not our job to fund elitism wrapped in a bow of social justice. We're the ones footing the bill while these schools continue to perpetuate a system that benefits only a select few.

If Harvard wants to play politics, then let them do it on their own dime. No—make that a $53 billion endowment! Why should our tax dollars support a university that prioritizes radical activism over education? It's time to put our money where it matters—into programs that actually benefit the community, like vocational training, affordable education, and mental health services.

So, what's the takeaway here? It's time to stop the funding for these institutions that have become hotbeds of radicalism and ignorance. Let's cut the check and let them fend for themselves. If they're so great, they'll find a way to thrive without our taxpayer dollars. And if they can't? Well, maybe that's a sign that they need to reevaluate their mission and their methods.

This isn't even worthy of a debate. It's time to put our hard-earned tax money to better use. Let's invest in institutions that actually contribute positively to society rather than subsidize the hate-filled echo chambers that Ivy League schools have become. Enough is enough—let's stop the funding, now and forever.

And as for those who think cutting off funding will harm education? Let me remind you that the best education comes from engaging with a variety of viewpoints, not just the ones that fit neatly into a leftist agenda. Real education is about challenging ideas, thinking critically, and preparing students for the complexities of the real world. If Harvard and its peers can't provide that, then they don't deserve a dime of our money.

It's time to demand accountability and transparency from these institutions. It's time to put the pressure on and say, "Enough is enough!" No more funding for hate, no more funding for ignorance, and no more funding for elitism. The future of education should be in the hands of those who truly value knowledge and understanding, not in the hands of those who wield it as a weapon against dissent. Let's cut the check and make a statement that echoes through the halls of these universities: we're done playing games.

◆ 17 ◆

FATHERHOOD

BEING OUT ON THE ROAD a lot, meeting people after shows, you really get a sense of what's happening in America. I love talking to folks, hearing their stories, and sometimes even meeting their kids. Whenever I meet someone's child, my mind immediately flashes back, thinking about what my kids are doing at that very moment. I don't share a lot about my kids because I want their lives to remain private, but I did want to address them in this book.

When people tell me I'm a great father, I chuckle a bit because, honestly? I'm a terrible father. A good father never would've had his children in the way that I did. It's not their fault, but I think I need to own that. I don't want my children to think their worth is tied to physical relationships. There was a time in my life where I thought that was the answer for everything, and it's a dangerous way to live.

I've seen the struggles of parenting from a unique angle. I've evolved from being mad at the world, blaming everyone else, to accepting that we all have our paths in this life. When things don't go as planned, you have two choices: wallow in it and use it as a crutch for the rest of your life, or rise above it. I've heard guys say, "Oh, she trapped me," or "These kids aren't mine." Let me tell you something: if you're a powerful man, how can a woman trap you? You chose to let it happen.

Once you graduate from that bullshit and start wearing your grown-man hat, you accept the challenges that come with being a father. My goal has always been to make sure my kids have everything they need and can follow their dreams, no matter the emotional, mental, or financial toll it takes on me. And just to be clear, I'm not talking about spoiling them. I don't buy gifts to say sorry, or shower them with material things.

There's a certain sacrifice you have to make as a man to provide for and take care of your children, and I'm doing that. But the downside? You don't get all the time that normal fathers get. It's hard when you have three kids living in three different states. I appreciate the effort it takes, but sometimes you get mad and upset—like, "Why can't I be there for them?" You weather the storm of their emotions, too, especially when they start talking about new dads or new families. It's not their fault; you just have to be there for them, even when it feels like it's tearing you apart inside.

You know, there's not a lot of guys writing books about responsibly taking care of three kids by three different mothers. Maybe Dr. Spock could've helped us out with that, but he didn't. So, you figure it out as you go along. I've got my ten-year-old now, and I'm in a solid relationship, but there are still those moments that make you wonder—are your kids sad that you have a life outside of them? Do they have a right to be mad, and how do you want them to be a part of it?

What does it even mean to be a good father? You protect your kids, provide for them, and give them every opportunity to be better than you were. You want to shield them from the mistakes you made. But then you also need to live your life. It's a balancing act that can feel impossible sometimes. I don't have a father or a grandfather or an uncle to call and ask for advice on how to navigate this. If I called my biological father, he wouldn't even know the names of my kids, let alone have anything helpful to say.

There's a certain shame in that, and I hate saying it because I am *not* ashamed of any of my children. But I do feel a sense of shame about the choices I made that led to their existence. It's important to accept accountability for that. I've got three gifts out of my past mistakes, but it's not something I'd recommend to anyone. No one should have to go through that.

I've stayed at jobs I didn't want because through them I was able to provide for my family. People ask, "Where's your dignity?" Let me tell you, if you're a father with mouths to feed, you don't get to have dignity. You can't just walk away because you personally don't like a situation. You have to swallow that pride and keep pushing through.

But as they grow older, the reality is they need you less and less. The FaceTimes get shorter, the text messages dwindle, and the visits become less frequent. You start waiting for the day when they're going to blame you. You know it's coming. They're going to demand to know why you made certain choices, especially when it comes to their mother. They won't care about your backstory; you're the man, and you have to answer for it.

And let me tell you, it hurts. I see it in my daughter's eyes when she gets upset and doesn't want to talk to me, especially when I try to enforce rules or set expectations. They'll turn it back on you, asking, "What about you?" It's heartbreaking because you realize you've let them down. Whether it's a failed marriage or a bad relationship, you've let them down. You have to own that, too.

So, when I hear people say, "You're a good dad," I just think, "The verdict's still out." The only ones who can tell me if I'm a good dad are my four kids. I hope I get to that point where they'll understand that *they* were not mistakes. They deserve to have come into this world under better circumstances, but they're here now. We're making the best of it, and we're continuing to learn and grow.

But I completely understand if my children hate me, or if they're angry with me. Worse than hate is indifference. If they're mad, there's a chance for reconciliation. They can come around. But if they're indifferent? That's the real killer. When you call and ask how their day was, and they respond with "It was fine," it cuts like a knife. You want to say, "You ungrateful brat," but they're not. I was the one who was disrespectful.

You have to own your choices and understand that there aren't always happy endings. You do the best with what you've got. One thing I've learned is that the worst thing I can do is try to be my kids' friend. I can't think of them as friends, in the sense that I can't be mad at them; I have to be the father they need. They might hate me at times, and they'll see me on TV whenever they flip through the channels, but I'm on the other side of the country a lot.

There's going to be a reckoning, and I'm preparing for it. I know that talk is coming, and it might involve three different conversations or just one big one. It could be a letter, or it could be them saying, "I don't want to know you." I can only speak from my experiences. I made decisions to move on from my family because it wasn't good for me, and it wasn't good for them, either.

But if my child says, "I don't want you in my life anymore, Dad," I will still make sure they have everything they need from afar. They're still my responsibility, even if they despise me or blame me. That's why it's hard to hear, "You're a good dad." They deserve better, and I'm working every day to ensure they have a better future.

Through my recklessness, I've lived up to every stereotype about a Black athlete, but there's an opportunity for redemption. I've dedicated my life to making sure my children don't go without. It's not a penance; it's an honor. Even if I'm standing next to their mom at their graduations, and they run to hug her first, I can't be bitter or angry.

I made the best out of a tough decision. The important thing is that they can run and hug their mom, or me, at their graduations, their sporting events, whatever it is. You shouldn't look for praise; you should just do what's right. I didn't do it the right way; I didn't marry one person and build a perfect family. But it's my family, and it's not the way it was drawn up in anyone's playbook.

I make the best of it. My last breath will be about making sure my kids are okay. Every time I get tired, frustrated, or feel passed over, I remember those four people who count on me for everything. So, you smile, you push on, and you be the dad they need. Fatherhood is tough, but it's like a knighthood. There will be battles and scars, but you show up every day, punch that clock, work that extra hour, train longer, and do what you have to do because they're counting on you.

And sometimes that can be the greatest inspiration in the world. But I 1,000 percent wish I had done things better before they were here. Maybe I'm overthinking it, but then again, maybe that's just the reality of fatherhood. Everyone's making babies, but not everyone thinks it through. I'm not ashamed of my kids; I love them. I love hearing their laughter, seeing their ideas come to life.

It's amazing to see pieces of you in them. I catch myself grinning when I see a little bit of my sense of humor in them, or one of my facial expressions. Those moments are precious. You don't get many of them, and you have to cherish them. You have to live in the moment. Don't just grab your phone to record it; enjoy it.

You know, one of the greatest movies of all time is *Blade Runner*. At the end, Rutger Hauer's character talks about the moments he's seen, and he says you must cherish them because they can be gone like tears in the rain. That's how I feel when I spend time with my kids. So, you won't see me plastering everything on social media to prove I'm a good dad. I'm too busy being in the moment with them.

And maybe that's right or wrong, but it's my belief system. I think it's right, and I'm okay with that. I'm not perfect, but I'm trying to do my best, and that's the most important thing a father can do.

◆ 18 ◆

GASLIGHTING

YOU'VE PROBABLY HEARD THE TERM "gaslighting" thrown around a lot, especially when citizens were trying to make sense of the madness coming out of DC. But what does it really mean?

First off, "gaslighting" isn't just some trendy term; it's rooted in a 1938 stage play that became a 1944 film called *Gaslight*. The story's about a guy who manipulates his wife into thinking she's going crazy by dimming the lights and messing with her reality. It's a classic case of psychological manipulation, and it's a perfect metaphor for what we saw during the Biden administration.

When that administration was in power, it felt like they were running a psychological operation on the American people. You had them telling us that inflation was "transitory" while we were all staring at skyrocketing prices at the grocery store. It was like being in a toxic relationship where your partner insists the sky is green and you're losing your mind for believing it's blue. That's gaslighting, plain and simple.

And please, this wasn't just some isolated incident. It was a full-on strategy. Every time they spun a narrative that contradicted reality, they were playing mind games with us. If you dared to question the narrative, suddenly you were labeled a conspiracy theorist or part of the "misinformation" crowd. It was frustrating as hell, and it left a lot of us feeling like we were losing grip on our own understanding of what was true.

The Biden administration had a knack for twisting facts and bending the truth. They had the media on speed dial, and social media platforms were more than happy to amplify their message. It was like a concerted effort to make sure we bought into their version of reality, even when it was clearly askew. You'd see politicians denying statements they made just days prior, and you started to wonder if you were the crazy one for remembering how it actually went down.

But this isn't just about Biden. It's a game that's been played by politicians for ages, but during his time in office, it felt like we were in a crash course on gaslighting. It was infuriating to watch.

So, what's the takeaway? Don't let them mess with your head. Keep your instincts sharp. If it feels off, it probably is. The term "gaslighting" isn't just some buzzword; it's a reminder to stay alert and not let anyone manipulate your perception of reality. We need to call it out for what it is. It's time to stop doubting ourselves and start questioning those who are trying to pull the wool over our eyes. The truth matters, and it's about time we reclaim it.

◆ 19 ◆

BILL MAHER, KID ROCK, AND THE DINNER THAT SHOOK THE LEFT

YOU MAY REMEMBER NOT TOO long ago when comedian Bill Maher decided to have dinner with none other than Donald Trump. And guess who played matchmaker for this little rendezvous? Kid Rock. Yeah, you heard me right. Kid Rock. When you've got a rock star putting together presidential meetings to build bridges, you know we're living in a truly special time, ha!

But my problem with what Bill Maher did isn't that he attended the dinner—it's what he did afterward. He went to the White House, had what seemed like a good time, and then scurried back to his platform, only to start backpedaling like he was on a ten-speed bike going downhill. The left came for him hard, and instead of standing his ground, he started throwing out all kinds of excuses, like a kid caught with his hand in the cookie jar.

Now, I can't get inside Bill Maher's head to figure out why he accepted that invite. Maybe he was looking for that Elon Musk-level push—by push, I mean the kind that gets the

American people buzzing. You know, Trump got all kinds of attention, and while it wasn't always good, let's face it: attention is attention. Maher probably thought he'd be the one sparking a conversation, stirring the pot. But I think he overestimated himself. He thought this monumental dinner would be the talk of the town, and instead, he ended up with egg on his face.

He came back from that dinner, and that's when I feel he really misplayed his hand. Instead of just telling it like it was—an entertaining evening with a gracious host—he tried to play both sides of the fence. He took the route of the typical leftist who can't commit to anything. You know, the kind of person who says, "Oh, I'm all for unity, but I'm not really sure about that guy." It's like he wanted to impress his liberal buddies while still trying to appear open-minded. But let's be honest: Maher wasn't being open-minded; he was being cowardly.

Trump is a gracious host, a fantastic conversationalist, and respectful in one-on-one settings. You sit down with him, and you start to understand the man behind the headlines. I've had my fair share of interactions with him, and I can tell you, it's a whole different experience than what you see on TV. After spending time with him, you might just find yourself owing him an apology for all those snarky comments you made in the past. I know I did!

So, what does Maher do? He goes back to his show, and instead of talking about how pleasant that dinner was, he starts hedging his bets and throwing out backhanded compliments. "Well, it was just one night, so I don't know...." Really? You went to the White House for dinner with the president of the United States, and that's your takeaway? It's like he was caught in a trap, trying to appease the very audience that would rather burn him in effigy than admit that Trump might not be the devil incarnate they've painted him to be.

And this is where it gets a little ridiculous. Maher's behavior reminded me of someone who has spent their whole life talking smack about a group of people, only to find themselves at dinner with one of them and suddenly acting like they're best friends. You know the type: they've spent years saying, "Oh, I could never hang out with them," and then they sit down at the table and say, "Hey, they're not that bad, guys!"

It's disingenuous, and it reeks of insincerity. If Maher really wanted to bridge the gap, he should have owned his experience. He should have said, "You know what? I had a great time. Trump is a fascinating guy, and maybe we need to have more conversations like this." But instead, he tried to play it safe, and in doing so, he lost all credibility.

This isn't just about Maher; it's a microcosm of the larger problem we're facing in our society today. We've got people who are so terrified about what their friends might think that they'll bend over backward to appease them, even when it means sacrificing their own honesty. It's like a social disease, and Maher caught it big time.

But let's not forget about Kid Rock, the man behind this historic dinner. The fact that Kid Rock was the one bringing Trump and Maher together is a testament to the strange world we're living in. Kid Rock is a guy who has never been afraid to speak his mind, and he's not shy about straddling the line between the left and the right. That's the kind of spirit we need more of in this country—a willingness to break down barriers and have real conversations, no matter how uncomfortable they might be.

But then there's Maher, who had this golden opportunity to embrace that spirit and instead chose to retreat into the safety of his liberal safe space. He had a chance to say, "You know what? We can disagree, but we can also have a good time together." Instead, he served up a buffet of excuses to justify why he didn't feel comfortable embracing the experience he just had.

So, what does this mean for the rest of us? It means we need to take a lesson from this situation. We can't be afraid to engage with people we disagree with. We can't let the fear of backlash dictate our conversations. If Bill Maher had stepped up and said, "Hey, I had dinner with Trump, and it was great," he would have opened the door for others to do the same. Instead, he slammed that door shut and left it locked.

It's time for all of us to stop playing the game of political correctness and start having honest conversations. We need to push back against the culture of fear that's taken hold of our discourse. We need to be willing to sit down at the table, share a meal, and discuss our differences without feeling the need to hedge our bets or sugarcoat our words.

And let's be honest—there's plenty of room for growth on both sides. The left needs to stop seeing every interaction with a conservative as some sort of betrayal, and the right needs to stop acting like every liberal is a snowflake. We're all human beings, and we need to start treating each other that way.

If we want to build bridges, we've got to be willing to take the first step. We've got to be willing to sit down, listen, and learn from each other. And we've got to stop making excuses for why we can't or shouldn't engage.

So, here's a message to Bill Maher: next time you find yourself at a dinner table with someone who might not share your views, don't backtrack later. Own the experience. Embrace it. You might just find that there's more to the conversation than you thought. And maybe, just maybe, you'll inspire others to do the same.

It's time to stop playing games and start having real conversations. Because if we don't, we're just going to keep spinning our wheels, stuck in the same old patterns of division and distrust.

So, here's to more dinners, more conversations, and more opportunities to build bridges. And here's to Kid Rock, the unlikely diplomat, for reminding us that sometimes it takes a rock star to shake things up in a world that desperately needs it. Let's keep the dialogue going—no more excuses, just honest conversations. That's how we make progress. That's how we unite. And that's how we move forward as a nation.

◆ 20 ◆

THE FINAL BOW OF BLACK LIVES MATTER

2024. THE YEAR BLACK LIVES Matter shuffled off this mortal coil. And you know what? Good riddance! We've had enough of the performative activism and the faux outrage that turned social media into a virtual parade of empty gestures. If 2020 was the year we all donned our "I care" badges, 2024 is the year we collectively threw them in the trash—right next to the "Black Square" filter.

Let's rewind a bit. Remember when BLM was the hottest hashtag on the block? Celebrities were taking knees, brands were slapping "Black Lives Matter" on everything from sneakers to salad dressing, and politicians were showing up in kente cloth like they'd just discovered the African continent last Tuesday. It was the age of "woke," a time when even your grandma was reposting about police brutality while knitting her "Black Lives Matter" scarf. But these days, what do we see? A collective yawn.

The truth is, like a sitcom that overstayed its welcome, the movement ran out of steam. The world moved on, and BLM, once a cultural juggernaut, has become an outdated meme. The statues came down, the hashtags trended, and then—

poof!—the momentum evaporated faster than a snowflake in the Sahara.

You see, the 2020 protests were fueled by raw emotion—an outpouring of grief, rage, and a desperate need for justice after the murder of George Floyd. It was a moment that ignited a firestorm of activism, drawing people from all walks of life into the streets. But as the summer of protests faded and the leaves began to fall, so did the energy. The media moved on to the next big story, and with it, the fervor for sustained change seemed to fizzle out.

What followed was a wave of corporate virtue signaling that would make any seasoned activist cringe. Companies began to roll out "diversity initiatives" faster than you could say "check the box." But let's be honest: those initiatives were like putting a fresh coat of paint on a crumbling building. Sure, it looked good for a moment, but you can't fix structural racism with a few more Black faces in the boardroom. It's like trying to fix a leaky faucet with a Band-Aid. In the end, it's just corporate window dressing.

The BBC's head of creative diversity, Joanna Abeyie, left after a year and a half, citing a lack of autonomy and influence. She loved the job, she says, but that wasn't enough. "These roles can become untenable when autonomy, influence, and decision-making is minimal to absent," she wrote. Sounds like a fun gig, right? You get to sit in the corner of the office with a fancy title while the real decisions are made elsewhere. If you feel like a decorative plant in a corner office, it's time to pack your bags!

And shockingly, it turns out that corporations aren't interested in actually changing the status quo. Who would have thought? Diversity, equity, and inclusion roles became the corporate equivalent of the "will call" ticket line—lots of waiting, not much happening. It seems that when push came to shove, the bottom line trumped any noble quest for equity. The overall impression is of organizations assuming that this would be easy and would not require proper budgets or uncomfortable transparency about salaries, seniority of roles, and who ultimately calls the shots and makes the big decisions.

The backlash was swift and fierce. Right-wing groups took aim at diversity policies. Lawsuits popped up like weeds in a garden, targeting schools and businesses for making the audacious move of offering scholarships specifically for Black students. I mean, can you imagine? A scholarship named after George Floyd? The horror! Apparently, acknowledging that systemic racism exists is now a partisan issue.

In the United States, the wave of anti-DEI (diversity, equity, and inclusion) lawsuits gained momentum, spurred on by a Supreme Court ruling against affirmative action. The legal landscape became a battleground, with right-wing groups eager to dismantle any semblance of progress made since 2020. They weren't just targeting universities; small businesses soon found themselves in the crosshairs, and thus began a cascade of corporations watering down their diversity and inclusion policies to avoid potential legal repercussions.

One of the organizations sued for policies seen as discriminatory was North Central University in Minneapolis. The Legal Insurrection Foundation, a far-right advocacy group, accused the university of violating the Civil Rights Act by reserving a scholarship for Black or African American students. The scholarship was the "George Floyd Memorial Scholarship." Can you believe it? Slicing through that scholarship was like saying, "How dare you acknowledge history? Just pretend everything is fine."

Meanwhile, there is a growing demonstration across the political spectrum that diversity and politics are two different things. Rishi Sunak's appointment as Prime Minister in the UK came with not only the same policies of crackdowns on strikes, protests, and even human rights laws, but also a bitter bonus of using the promotions of Black and brown people to positions of power to scold us. "We're here, aren't we?" Sunak says, living proof that you should stop griping about racism.

Whatever residual, misty-eyed longing there was for people of color to reach the highest offices was surely dashed by a brown multimillionaire endlessly bleating that he is here to "stop the boats." Personally, little has been more helpful in removing the scales from my eyes than the notion that Kemi Badenoch's rise is something to be celebrated.

As the movement began to fall apart, the conversations around it grew increasingly toxic. The term "woke" morphed into a pejorative, weaponized by those who felt threatened by any discussion of systemic racism. BLM quickly became shorthand for everything from anti-capitalism to a general disdain for traditional values. It was no longer about police reform or social justice; it became a catch-all for any and every grievance on the right. It was a perfect recipe for backlash, as people began to associate the movement with a host of radical ideas, none of which had anything to do with the original mission.

The once-unifying message of "Black Lives Matter" became a political grenade tossed in the culture wars. Instead of galvanizing a movement for change, it fueled division. Politicians on both sides seized the opportunity to score points. If you were against BLM, you were branded a racist. If you were for it, you were a radical. And in the end, everyone lost.

Even in the realm of education, the impact of the backlash was palpable. In the UK, Black Lives Matter was described as containing "partisan" political views that "must not be promoted to pupils," according to government guidance on political impartiality in classrooms. Teachers were left in a precarious position, unsure of how to engage students in meaningful discussions about race without running afoul of new regulations.

Meanwhile, in the United States, the growing wave of anti-Black Lives Matter sentiment led to legislation aimed at restricting discussions on race in schools. You know the drill: "Don't teach Critical Race Theory!" became the rallying cry, leaving educators scrambling to teach a complete history without offending anyone. The irony is delicious—these same lawmakers often tout the importance of a well-rounded education, yet they're the first to stifle conversations that might challenge the status quo.

So here we are, in the aftermath of the BLM frenzy, staring at the ashes of what was once a vibrant movement. It's not that the issues of racial injustice have vanished; they're still lurking in the shadows, waiting for the next wave of genuine activism to rise up. But for now, BLM is like that old flip phone in your drawer—obsolete and forgotten, yet somehow still taking up space.

But let's not mistake the death of Black Lives Matter for the end of the fight for racial equality. The world still needs activists, thinkers, and doers who are committed to real change. The key is to strip away the performative nonsense and get down to the real work of addressing racial inequality. It's time to stop playing dress-up and actually roll up our sleeves. Because if we've learned anything from this roller-coaster ride, it's that real change doesn't come from hashtags or trendy slogans—it comes from hard, uncomfortable conversations and actions that may actually cost us something.

The death of Black Lives Matter as we knew it isn't a tragedy; it's an opportunity. An opportunity to engage in those difficult conversations we've been avoiding for so long. An opportunity to rethink our approach to activism and to focus on the issues that truly matter. So, let's raise a glass to the demise of Black Lives Matter as we knew it. Here's to rebirth, to real conversations, and to the hope that the next movement will be about substance, not style.

It's time for a renaissance in activism, one that goes beyond hashtags and social media trends. One that values genuine dialogue and meaningful action over performative gestures. Let's dig in and start the real work, because if there's one thing we've learned from the fall of BLM, it's that the fight for racial justice is far from over. It's time to reclaim the narrative, to rebuild the movement, and to do it in a way that's authentic, inclusive, and—dare I say it?—effective.

◆ 21 ◆

SHELL GAMES AND CONSEQUENCES

AS I SIT DOWN TO write this chapter, I can't help but reflect on the absurdity that has become American politics. It's a chaotic spectacle, a bad reality show where the stakes are alarmingly high. But what unfolded on this particular day involving former FBI Director James Comey takes the cake as one of the most reckless and irresponsible acts I've ever witnessed. Not just in politics, but in our society.

Here's the lowdown: Comey, a man who once held one of the most powerful positions in law enforcement, decided to share a post on Instagram displaying seashells arranged in the numbers "86-47." He captioned it, "Cool shell formation on my beach walk." Now, let's be real—if you're a former FBI director sharing a post that can be interpreted as a threat against a sitting president, you need to have your head examined.

For those who might be a bit slow on the uptake, "eighty-six" is slang for getting rid of someone, sometimes even "to kill." It's a term that's been around long enough to penetrate the political lexicon, and it's not a leap to think that people might take that shell arrangement as something sinister. And "forty-seven"—well, Donald Trump is the forty-seventh president. Donald Trump Jr. didn't mince words when he accused Comey of "calling for my dad to be murdered." And honestly, how do you argue against that? When you have a former FBI director throwing around numbers that carry such heavy implications, it's not just a misstep; it's a serious issue.

Comey quickly deleted the post, claiming he had no idea that his numbers could be interpreted as a violent message. Seriously? A guy with his background should know better. If you're in a position of power and influence, especially with the political climate we're in today, you'd think Comey would exercise a little more caution. But instead, he threw caution to the wind and left us all wondering what the hell he was thinking.

What's even better is that some Republicans are actually calling for Comey to face consequences for his actions. Good! We should absolutely hold him accountable. Homeland Security Secretary Kristi Noem announced that her department and the Secret Service were investigating this so-called "threat." And you know what? They should be. We live in a time when threats against public figures, especially the president, are a real and present danger. It's not just a political game anymore; it's a matter of life and death.

The Secret Service took it seriously too, stating they "vigorously investigate anything that can be taken as a potential threat against our protectees." Good. They should treat rhetoric like this with the seriousness it deserves. If we're going to protect our leaders, we need to take every potential threat seriously—especially when it comes from someone who should know better.

Let's recall the context here. Comey has been a thorn in Trump's side since day one. After being fired in 2017 while overseeing the investigation into Russian meddling in the 2016 election, he's made no secret of his disdain for the man in the Oval Office. So, when you see a post like this, it raises alarms. It's reckless and irresponsible, and it deserves to be punished.

But let's take a moment to flip the script. Can you imagine if the tables were turned? Picture this: a high-ranking official in the Trump administration posts something similar—an Instagram photo with numbers arranged in a way that could be interpreted as a threat against a Democrat. Do you think the media would shrug it off? Of course not! We all know the media would be in a frenzy, whipping up outrage like it's the last drop of gasoline before a storm.

The headlines would scream: "Trump Official Sends Ominous Message!" "Threatening Rhetoric from the Right!" You'd see every news outlet dissecting that post with the meticulousness of a forensic analyst. There would be calls for investigations, demands for resignations, and an outcry from politicians on both sides of the aisle. The public would be up in arms, and rightly so. In that case, the reaction would be swift and severe; but in this case, because it's Comey—a figure vilified by many in the Trump camp—there seems to be this strange reluctance to hold him accountable.

This double standard is infuriating. It exemplifies the hypocrisy that runs rampant in our political discourse. The left can throw accusations around without consequence, while the right is scrutinized under a microscope for every little thing. If Comey had made a similar post but was part of the Trump administration, I guarantee he would be facing far harsher backlash and possibly even criminal charges. But because he's perceived as a hero to some, he gets a pass.

Face it, the stakes are incredibly high. We live in a climate where there have been multiple assassination attempts against a sitting president. Given that context, Comey's actions aren't just a silly social media misstep; they're dangerous. They trivialize the very real threats that come with being in the public eye. It's not just about words; it's about the culture we're fostering—a culture where threats are laughed off and where the consequences are nonexistent for some but severe for others.

The fact that Comey was a former FBI director only amplifies the seriousness of this situation. He should know better. He should understand that his words carry weight, especially in an age where misinformation and violence can spread like wildfire. When you have someone with his experience making such a reckless move, it sends a message that it's okay to be irresponsible—that it's acceptable to engage in behavior that could be interpreted as a threat.

I don't care how you slice it; this is unacceptable. There should be zero tolerance for this kind of nonsense. Comey needs to be punished for his actions, and we must establish a standard that applies to everyone, regardless of political affiliation. If we allow this kind of behavior to slide, we're essentially giving a green light to more of the same.

And it's not just Comey. This mentality needs to be addressed across the board. In today's climate, politicians and public figures need to understand that their words matter and that the impact of their actions can have real-world consequences. There's no room for ambiguity when it comes to threats against anyone, let alone the president.

So, what should happen to Comey? It's simple: he needs to face repercussions for his reckless behavior. This isn't a partisan issue; it's about ensuring that everyone understands the gravity of their words and actions.

As we move forward, we need to demand accountability from our leaders. We should not tolerate a double standard in our political discourse. Whether you're a Democrat, Republican, or anything in between, you should be held to the same standard. It's time to stop playing games and start taking this seriously. If we don't start taking this seriously, we risk normalizing a culture where threats are treated as jokes and where accountability is a thing of the past.

Comey needs to understand that his words have weight, and in today's world, we simply can't afford to take threats lightly. Accountability is vital. As citizens, we must demand it from those in power, regardless of which side of the aisle they sit on. Because when we let things like this go unpunished, we're not just failing to uphold our values; we're setting a dangerous precedent for future generations.

The message must be clear: threats of any kind will not be tolerated, and those who make them will face the consequences. It's time to raise the bar and ensure that everyone understands the stakes involved in our political discourse. We owe it to ourselves, our leaders, and our country.

◆ 22 ◆

THE "BIG BOY PRESS CONFERENCE" —A COMEDY OF ERRORS

AS I SIT HERE WRITING, Donald Trump is well into his second term, and the chatter surrounding Biden's incompetence has reached a fever pitch. But the real story isn't just about Biden's flailing in the spotlight; it's about the cover-up that kept most Americans completely in the dark about who was actually running the country. Let's not beat around the bush: it's obvious to anyone with half a brain that Biden's cognitive abilities have seen better days. But as the walls began to close in on him, the White House had to scramble to put Biden out in front of cameras, hoping to convince the public that he could still string together a coherent sentence.

Enter what became known as the "big boy press conference." A couple of weeks after Biden's legendary train wreck of a debate with Trump in Atlanta, the White House decided it was time to prove to the world—or at least attempt to gaslight them—that Joe was still capable of functioning as a president. They set the stage for this press conference, which was supposed to be a triumphant return to form for the leader of the free world after that disastrous debate. The stakes were higher than a kite on a windy day, and the pressure was palpable.

Now, if you thought the name "big boy press conference" was just a quirky title, think again. The White House communications team, led by Karine Jean-Pierre, actually referred to it as that with a straight face. I mean, come on! They were essentially admitting to the American people that they were praying their president could finally act like a fully functioning adult. It sounded less like a serious political event and more like a toddler showing off his new shoelaces. "Look, Ma! I can tie my shoes!"

For the record, Biden survived his big boy press conference only because the bar wasn't even set low; there wasn't really any bar left to speak of anymore. The expectations were so minimal that being even slightly better than his performance in the Trump debate qualified as a victory in the eyes of the White House. They trumpeted, "Joe is back!" But taken on its own, it was simply another forgettable bit of mediocrity in a less-than-lackluster political career.

Now, let's take a moment to rewind the tape back to that Atlanta debate, where the world watched as Biden struggled to keep up with a more agile Trump. This was a moment that should have sent alarm bells ringing throughout the Democratic Party. Yet, what did we see immediately after the debate? Jill Biden welcomed her husband with open arms, showering him with praise as if he had just delivered a Nobel Prize-winning speech. "Didn't the president do a great job? Yes!" she declared to supporters gathered at the hotel, a gleam of pride in her eyes.

And after a brief pause, the crowd began chanting, "Four more years!" Meanwhile, Jill continued her cheerleading, exclaiming, "Joe, you did such a great job! You answered every question, you knew all the facts." Then, as if on cue, she turned to the crowd and asked, "And what did Trump do?" The response was a unison shout of "Lie!"

This display was a textbook example of infantilization, a moment when we were all reminded that Jill Biden was more than just a supportive spouse; she was a woman who seemed to be coddling her husband in a way that left many of us shaking our heads. We should have known right then and there that it was all over. Instead of acknowledging the reality of the situation, she chose to wrap Joe in a bubble of denial, proclaiming his performance a success when, in truth, it was anything but.

The media, for their part, didn't have the guts to call it out. They waited, instead, for the "big boy press conference" to help salvage his campaign. They knew the stakes were high, and they were just as complicit in this charade. The infantilization continued, as they treated the press conference like some kind of milestone—an opportunity to reassure the American people that their president could still hold it together, even if only for a few moments.

In the lead-up to this highly anticipated event, whispers of doubt swirled around Biden's candidacy. Even some of his strongest political allies were starting to question whether he should run again in 2024. And can you blame them? With every misstep, the notion that Biden might be losing his grip on reality became harder to ignore. Hollywood heavyweight George Clooney, who had once held a glitzy fundraiser for Biden, publicly called on him not to seek re-election. Ouch! That was a knife twist from a guy who was supposed to be in the president's corner.

Then there was Nancy Pelosi, who didn't exactly offer a glowing endorsement. She merely suggested that Biden should make a decision after the NATO summit. Translation: "Let's see how this goes before I put my neck on the line for you." Even Senator Peter Welch from Vermont joined the chorus of Democrats urging Biden to step aside. The message was clear: People were worried, and rightly so.

As the clock ticked down to the big moment, Biden's solo press conference was overshadowed by an air of desperation. His previous appearances had been tightly controlled affairs, with joint statements alongside foreign leaders where each was given just two questions. Critics accused the White House of hiding the effects of age and incompetence from the public, and honestly, who could blame them?

When Biden finally took the stage for the "big boy press conference," the expectations were so low that even a half-decent performance would have qualified as a victory. But remember the setting: a Washington, DC, conference center, where the pressure was on for Biden to prove he could handle what had become a rare unscripted moment in his presidency.

As he shuffled to the podium, the world held its breath—well, sort of. The press pool, eager to catch any slip-up, was ready. The moment he opened his mouth, it was clear he was treading water, trying to stay afloat in a sea of his own making. There was a sense of urgency in the air, a collective hope that he wouldn't embarrass himself further.

And sure, he managed to string a few sentences together. But let's be honest: it was like praising a toddler for finally using the potty. "Congratulations, Joe! You did it!" The truth is, he was basic. He was a little bit better than he had been in the Trump debate, which, in the eyes of the White House communications team, was enough to declare victory. But in reality, it was just another lackluster performance in a less-than-lackluster political career.

In the aftermath of the press conference, the White House continued to refer to it as Biden's "big boy press conference," as if they were trying to convince the American people that this was a monumental achievement. But in reality, it was just a desperate attempt to distract from the chaos and confusion surrounding Biden's presidency. The fact that they kept using that phrase only served to highlight how far the administration had fallen.

What's fascinating is that the White House wasn't just trying to win over the public; they were also trying to reassure themselves. It was a clear acknowledgment of the reality they were dealing with: Biden's cognitive decline wasn't just a rumor; it was a fact. And by labeling this press conference as "big boy," they inadvertently exposed their own fears about his ability to lead.

Watching the event unfold, I couldn't help but think about the absurdity of it all. Here we had a president who was supposed to be leading the free world, and yet he was being celebrated for simply showing up and not completely collapsing on stage. It was a sad state of affairs, and it illustrated perfectly the dysfunction that had permeated the Biden administration.

The media, of course, had a field day with the press conference. They dissected every word, every pause, every stutter. Some praised him for simply managing to get through it, while others pointed out that it wasn't a real victory; it was merely a reflection of how low the bar had been set. The headlines ranged from "Biden's Comeback?" to "A Sigh of Relief?"

It was clear that the narrative being spun was more about survival than success.

But please remember the real implications of this performance—or lack thereof. The fact that the White House had to resort to such desperate measures spoke volumes about the state of the administration. They were trying to sell the idea that Biden could still lead, but the reality was much harsher. The American people were left to sift through this chaos, trying to figure out who was really in charge. Biden's cognitive decline wasn't going to disappear, and the doubts surrounding his leadership would only continue to grow.

"The big boy press conference" was, in many ways, a metaphor for the Biden presidency itself—an exercise in trying to appear competent while the reality was anything but. We need leaders who can rise to the occasion, who can face the challenges courageously, and who can inspire confidence in their ability to lead. But what we got instead was a half-hearted attempt by desperate staffers to convince us that everything was fine, when in fact the wheels were falling off the Biden presidency.

"The big boy press conference" served as both a punchline and a wake-up call. It was a reminder that, in politics, the absurd often becomes the norm. The American people deserve better than a leader who can only manage to tie his shoes when the cameras are on. We deserve a president who can navigate the complexities of governance with confidence, clarity, and, most importantly, competence. And until we get that, we'll be left with more "big boy" moments that only serve to highlight the glaring inadequacies of those in power.

◆ 23 ◆

AGE LIMITS ON CAPITOL HILL:

TIME FOR FRESH FACES

THE STATE OF OUR GOVERNMENT is like a bad wrestling match where the ref is blindfolded, and the only thing getting pinned is common sense. If you've been paying attention, you know that the past few years under Joe Biden have felt like watching a slow-motion train wreck.

Now, don't get me wrong—I'm not trying to pick on Biden just for the sake of it. This goes way beyond him. The issue we're staring down is much larger: age limits on Capitol Hill. Look around! We've got a bunch of folks up there in their late seventies and eighties, and the spectacle is becoming a real circus act. You know what I'm talking about. Nancy Pelosi? Chuck Schumer? They've been around longer than some of our history books. And let's not forget about some Republicans who've been hanging on like a bad smell—Mitch McConnell, anyone?

And while we're at it, look at Trump. He's in his late seventies, too. But he's an anomaly. Love him or hate him, the guy still has the energy and mental acuity of someone half his age.

You can see it in how he engages with people, how he speaks, and how he rallies his supporters. But the rest of these politicians? They need to look in the mirror and ask themselves if they're really serving the country or just holding onto power for dear life.

Let's get down to brass tacks: nearly 20 percent of House and Senate members are seventy or older, while just about 6 percent are under forty. That's right—20 percent of our lawmakers are pushing eighty, while only a tiny fraction of them represents the voices of young Americans. Meanwhile, the median age in the Senate is nearly sixty-five, with forty-nine members at least that old. Do we really think that's a recipe for progress? While most people look forward to retirement at sixty-five, these politicians treat their positions like they're some kind of lifetime membership in an exclusive club.

Now, I'm not saying we should kick everyone out the door at seventy. Sure, there's value in having experienced members of Congress, but that's no excuse to let octogenarians run the country. We have a minimum age requirement for Congress and the presidency because young people often lack maturity, experience, and a track record of trustworthiness. So why in the world can't we have a maximum age limit, too? Senility in our leaders can be just as dangerous as inexperience and lack of maturity.

Another thing: elderly politicians don't have as much skin in the game. They're making decisions that affect a generation of Americans who have fifty or more years ahead of them. But what do they care about the long-term consequences of their actions? They won't be around to live with the fallout from their poor decisions. This is a fundamental flaw in our system. When the old refuse to pass the torch, it stifles the growth and experience of those coming up behind them. Middle management can't gain upper management experience if the upper management refuses to retire!

Let's dig deeper into the psychology of aging leaders in politics. There's a phenomenon known as "confirmation bias," where individuals tend to favor information that confirms their existing beliefs. The longer someone has been in power, the more entrenched they become in their views. They might have started off with good intentions, but eventually, they fall into the trap of maintaining the status quo. They have their networks, their lobbyists, and their contributors, and they become reluctant to make waves. This stagnation can lead to policies that are outdated, irrelevant, and downright harmful.

And let's not pretend that the main priority of the current crop of elderly politicians is serving the public good. Many of them are in it for the power and the perks. They may have started with good intentions, but somewhere along the way, they got lost in their own self-importance. They've built their empires, and now they're clinging to them like they're life rafts.

Let's also talk about the economic impact of having older politicians in power. These people often have their pensions, their investments, and their financial security already lined up. They don't have the same urgency to create policies that benefit the younger generation struggling to make ends meet. They're not looking at the world through the same lens. When was the last time a politician in their eighties had to worry about paying student loans or affording a first home? Exactly. It's a disconnect that's glaring and unacceptable.

Again, I'm not saying we should push out every older politician simply because they're older. That's not the point.

There are plenty of wise and experienced individuals who can contribute positively. But it's not just about them anymore. It's about us—the American people. And we need to set some boundaries.

It's simple: if you're not growing, you're dying. And if DC wants to keep up with the times, it needs to start making room for the next generation. You want to talk about the future? That's where we need to focus. We need leaders who can see beyond their own lifetimes and consider the long-term impact of their decisions. If we allow people who are nearing the end of their lives to dictate the future for those who have decades ahead of them, we're setting ourselves up for failure. How many times have we seen politicians cling to power, only to hinder progress? It's like a bad reality show that just won't get canceled.

When you look at the current state of affairs, it's clear that this isn't just about age; it's about responsibility. Let's remind these aging politicians that it's not about them; it's about us. We can't let them hog the spotlight while the next generation waits in the wings. With the average age of members of Congress now skewing older, we're missing out on innovative ideas and fresh approaches that younger leaders can bring to the table. The old guard may have their place in history, but it's time to pass the torch. It's time we start embracing the potential of that new generation.

We need to demand that our leaders reflect the diversity and dynamism of the country they represent. We need leaders who are willing to listen to fresh and emerging voices, who can relate to the struggles of young Americans, and who understand the challenges we face. We deserve leaders who are in touch with our realities, who can relate to our struggles, and who are ready to fight for a better future.

A maximum age limit would encourage a healthier turnover in leadership. It would create opportunities for younger leaders to step in and bring fresh ideas to the table, while also ensuring that those in power are still engaged with the issues affecting the population they serve. Imagine a Congress filled with dynamic young leaders who can relate to the struggles of everyday Americans. They'd understand the challenges of student debt, housing affordability, and job security because they're living it! They'd challenge the status quo and work across party lines to get things done.

So, let's get serious about this. We need to advocate for change and push for age limits in Congress. There are young people out there with innovative ideas, energy, and passion. They're ready to tackle the issues that matter to us now. But as long as the old guard refuses to step aside, those young voices remain stifled.

We can—and must—do better. It's time to break the cycle. It's time to shake things up and make room for fresh perspectives. Let's demand a government that truly represents all of us—not just the older generation that's been stuck in the same old patterns.

So, here's the challenge: let's start talking about age limits. Age limits on Capitol Hill are not just a good idea; they are necessary for the health and future of our democracy. Let's advocate for change and push back against the idea that being in your eighties qualifies you to run the country. The time is now for a new generation of leaders. Our future is at stake, and it's time to claim it!

24

THE GREAT RETIREMENTS:
A SARCASTIC FAREWELL TO LEFTIST LINGUISTICS

AH, THE SWEET, SWEET SOUND of a second Trump presidency—a time when the nation can finally start addressing the real problems at hand. I mean, let's be honest: we've been drowning in a sea of leftist jargon for way too long. It's like a bad hangover that just won't quit. But fear not, because with the dawn of this new era, we're getting ready to retire some of the most obnoxious phrases that have taken root in our society like weeds in an untended garden. You know, the ones that made you want to roll your eyes so hard you could see your own brain? Grab your popcorn.

First up on the chopping block is "mansplain." Ah yes, the beloved term that implies that if a man explains something, he's automatically condescending and patronizing. I don't know about you, but I've had my fair share of people who can mansplain regardless of their gender. It's not a gender issue; it's a personality flaw. Some folks just can't resist the urge to talk down to others, regardless of whether they sport a beard or a ponytail. So, let's retire this term and focus on the real problem: condescension, which—wait for it—can come from anyone!

Next, we have the "male gaze." This is the concept that women are viewed through a lens of objectification by men. Let me tell you, this cliché is like a bad sitcom that keeps getting renewed for another season. The male gaze has become an all-purpose scapegoat for everything from Hollywood's portrayal of women to the way a guy looks at you across the bar. Hello, everyone: not every compliment is a product of some patriarchal conspiracy. Sometimes, a glance is just a glance! We need to retire this phrase and start recognizing that, yes, sometimes people are just people, and attraction is part of the human experience.

Speaking of objectification, here's another gem we can toss into the retirement bin: "objectify." This term has been misused to the point that it's lost its meaning. Yes, objectification is a real issue, but it's not the end of the world. The reality is that we live in a society where physical attraction exists, and it's not always sinister. Let's face it: you might objectify a celebrity because they have a six-pack or killer cheekbones, but it doesn't mean you're plotting to turn them into a literal object. Let's dial it back and recognize when it's just harmless admiration.

Now we come to "non-binary." Look, I get it; gender can be fluid, and that's great! But can we stop trying to fit everyone into a label box? Non-binary people are valid, but so are people who identify as male or female. We don't need a separate term for every single variation of gender identity. It's like trying to create a menu at a restaurant that has five hundred different options. At some point, you just want a burger and fries, right? Let's simplify things and embrace the spectrum without drowning in a sea of labels.

And speaking of labels, don't forget "cisgender." This word is thrown around like beads at a Mardi Gras parade, but it's just a fancy way of saying you identify with the gender you were assigned at birth. Great! But does it really need its own term? How about we just call it "normal"? Oh wait, can't use that word anymore. "Cisgender" has become the new "vanilla," and it's time to retire it. Just be who you are without needing to slap a label on it.

Ah, "microaggression." The term that implies that every time someone accidentally says something that offends you, it's a calculated attack. Come on: not every offhand comment is meant to offend. Sometimes, people are just clueless. We've all been there, right? Instead of crying "microaggression," how about we take a deep breath, roll our eyes, and move on? We need to stop treating every little comment like it's a personal attack and start embracing a little resilience.

Now, let's talk about "safe space." This phrase has taken on a life of its own, fostering a culture of fragility that's more toxic than any troll on the internet. Safe spaces were originally meant to be places where marginalized individuals could feel secure and accepted. Great idea in theory, but what happened? They turned into cult camps, where only certain views are allowed. It's time to retire the term and embrace the real world, where discomfort is a part of growth.

Then there's "trigger warning." This term started with good intentions but has devolved into a way for people to avoid anything that doesn't fit their narrative. Here's a thought: instead of warning people about potential triggers, how about we encourage them to build some mental fortitude? Life is full of surprises, and sometimes they're not pleasant. Let's stop wrapping everyone in bubble wrap and encourage them to face the world with guts and honestly.

Finally, we have "heteronormative." This fancy word suggests that heterosexuality is the default, and anything else is abnormal. Can we retire this one, too? Because honestly, every relationship—regardless of orientation—has its own set of norms. Everyone's life is different, and lumping people into a singular category of "normal" is not only reductive but also harmful. Let's celebrate all types of love without boxing them into "normative" or "non-normative" categories.

So, there you have it. With Trump's second term, we're going to take a sledgehammer to the lexicon of leftist linguistics and start fresh. While some of these terms might have had noble origins, they've become the linguistic equivalent of an overcooked vegetable—nobody wants to eat that. We need to embrace a new vocabulary that focuses on understanding, resilience, and humor, because as we all know the world is a chaotic place, and we could all use a good laugh.

In this new era, let's retire the jargon that divides us and start using language that unites us. Life is too short to be offended by every little thing, so let's embrace the chaos, laugh a little harder, and remember that we're all just humans trying to figure it out.

◆ 25 ◆

STFU ABOUT HITLER, ALREADY

LET'S CUT THROUGH THE BULLSHIT, shall we? The next time you hear someone likening Donald Trump to Adolf Hitler, just know that they've officially entered the realm of the absurd. And the second you drop that name, you lose the argument. You might as well just wave a white flag and admit you've got nothing left to say. Why? Because invoking Hitler is not just a cheap shot; it's a lazy tactic that undermines any serious criticism you might have about Trump or the Republican Party. So let's put it to rest, once and for all.

First off, let's get one thing straight: Adolf Hitler was a mass murderer who orchestrated the systematic extermination of over six million Jews during the Holocaust. He didn't just have a few bad ideas; he executed a horrific plan that led to the deaths of millions of innocent people. The atrocities committed under his regime are well-documented and beyond comprehension. So when you throw around his name in a conversation about Donald Trump, you're not just making a poor analogy; you're trivializing one of the darkest chapters in human history.

Now, I get it. People get emotional about politics. They feel like they're fighting against something evil, and they want to draw parallels that make their case seem stronger. But there are no real parallels between Trump and Hitler. If you genuinely believe there are, then I'm sorry to say it, but you're the one who looks like an idiot.

Let's take a moment to remember what Hitler's master plan really was. His regime wasn't about merely criticizing the media or calling out "fake news." It was about establishing a totalitarian state where dissent was crushed, and anyone who opposed him was either silenced or exterminated. You think Trump's Social media rants are a sign of a dictator in the making? Please. Hitler didn't just have a bad day at the office; he unleashed the Gestapo—the secret police that terrorized anyone who dared to oppose him. His regime was about control—absolute control over every facet of life, from the media to the arts, to education, to personal freedoms.

The Nazis didn't just disagree with dissenters; they didn't just call them names. They rounded them up, sent them to concentration camps, and murdered them. So when someone says Trump is like Hitler because he criticizes the media, that's not just a stretch; it's a ludicrous insult to the memory of the millions who perished under Hitler's regime.

Now let's think about the media for a second. Sure, Trump has a contentious relationship with the press, but so what? He's not the first president to have a beef with journalists. The media has always been a punching bag for politicians, and the idea that Trump wants to lock up reporters in gulags is laughable. If you really think that's where we're headed, you need to get off your social media account and step out into the real world.

Before he ran for president, Trump was a darling of the media. He was a guest on every talk show and a headline in every tabloid. The Democrats loved him then—so why didn't they call him Hitler back when he was writing checks to their campaigns? Was it because he was a "good" kind of Hitler? The truth is, they didn't have a problem with him until he decided to run for office as a Republican. And then, suddenly, he became the embodiment of evil. Talk about hypocrisy.

Now, can we talk about real issues? You can certainly criticize Trump for his policies, his behavior, and the way he conducts himself in office. There's a treasure trove of legitimate arguments to be made against him. His immigration policies? Controversial. His handling of the COVID-19 pandemic? Open to scrutiny. His approach to international relations? Worth debating. But when you pull out the "H-word," you're not just changing the narrative; you're derailing it entirely.

Invoking Hitler doesn't strengthen your argument; it weakens it. It turns a serious conversation into a ridiculous shouting match. You want to talk about fascism? Let's do that. You want to discuss authoritarianism? I'm all in. But don't dilute those conversations with empty rhetoric that only serves to distract from the real issues.

Have you noticed that the left has an obsession with Hitler? It's like they've got a playbook that says, "Whenever in doubt, just call your opponent Hitler." Well, I have some bad news for them: it's not working. It's not clever, it's not smart; it's lazy. Instead of doing the hard work of crafting a compelling argument, they'd rather throw around the name of a dictator who was responsible for genocide. If you want to convince anyone of your point, invoking Hitler is not the way to go.

And let's not forget the hypocrisy of it all. If we're going to start throwing around comparisons, let's talk about the left's own history. Remember Stalin? He's responsible for the deaths of millions, as well. But you don't hear people on the left calling out each other for that, do you? No, it's always "Trump is Hitler," while they conveniently ignore the left's own bloody history.

Now here's the irony: when you think about who wanted to silence the opposition, who wanted to destroy the lives of people in disagreement, who wanted to stifle free speech and cancel any culture that didn't fall in lockstep with the party line—well, maybe it's time to look in the fucking mirror for a minute. I'm not going to be a hypocrite and tell you that you're Hitler for drawing those comparisons; but the very act of likening political opponents to a genocidal maniac is a tactic that seeks to silence those who don't agree with you. And isn't that just a little bit...convenient? When you throw around terms like "Nazi" or "Gestapo" to describe those you disagree with, you're invoking a legacy of brutality that is not only misleading but dangerously dismissive of the actual historical atrocities committed under those regimes.

If you want to engage in serious political debate, then do just that—engage. But when you resort to hyperbolic comparisons that reflect more on your own inability to articulate a nuanced argument, it's time to reconsider your approach. Instead of stifling dissent with such inflammatory rhetoric, maybe take a step back and ask yourself: who really embodies the spirit of silencing opposition here?

So why does this matter? Because when we trivialize the horrendous acts committed by Hitler, we risk losing sight of the lessons that history has taught us. We need to learn from the past, not throw it around like a cheap party favor whenever we're feeling upset. Real comparisons deserve real scrutiny, and throwing Hitler's name into the mix dilutes the gravity of actual historical atrocities.

We should be passionate about our beliefs and engage in robust debates. But we should be able to criticize our leaders without resorting to hysterical hyperbole. If you care about the truth, then you owe it to yourself—and to the memory of those who suffered under regimes like Hitler's—to maintain a level of seriousness in your discourse.

So, the next time you hear someone invoke Hitler while discussing Donald Trump, just shake your head and move on. Understand that they've lost the argument before it even began. If you want to engage in serious political discourse, do it without the cheap shots. Criticize, debate, and argue your points, but leave Hitler out of it.

Because when you bring him up, you're not making a compelling case. You're just proving that you've got no idea what you're talking about. And that's the real tragedy here. So shut the fuck up about Hitler already, and let's have a real conversation about the issues that matter. Real dialogue is what we need, not the empty rhetoric of historical comparisons that only serve to distract and divide us. Let's do better.

◆ 26 ◆

STFU ABOUT HITLER, ALREADY:

PART TWO

AS I SIT HERE WORKING on this book, I still find myself surrounded by a cacophony of headlines and social media posts where well-known figures are invoking Hitler and related themes, and it's enough to make your head spin. By the time you read this, I suspect these absurdities will still be fresh in your mind. Just recently, former Bill Clinton adviser James Carville had the audacity to suggest that those cooperating with President Trump's administration might be treated like Nazi collaborators after World War II. Seriously? This is the level of discourse we've sunk to?

Then there's Illinois Governor JB Pritzker, who, during his state of the state budget address, drew parallels between Trump's populist agenda and the rise of the Nazis prior to World War II. This isn't just rhetoric; it's a blatant misunderstanding of both history and current events. And just a couple of days ago, former Vice President Al Gore decided to join the clown parade, comparing the Trump administration to Hitler's Third Reich.

And then there's the usual parade of D-listers: Kamala Harris often calls Trump a fascist, while actor Robert De Niro has made it his life's mission to warn us about the looming specter of Hitler and Nazis at every opportunity. Honestly, if I had a dollar for every time someone invoked Hitler to make a political point, I could fund a campaign to educate these folks on the actual historical context of their comparisons.

But one of the worst offenders in this absurdity parade? Larry David, with his "satirical" opinion piece in *The New York Times* titled "My Dinner with Adolf." In this ill-conceived piece, he took aim at Bill Maher's recent dinner with Trump. Now, I'll get to Maher's dinner elsewhere in the book, but let me focus for a moment on David, a guy I genuinely think is funny. What he did wasn't funny or clever; it was just disappointing—an ignorant, out-of-touch, foolhardy move.

David's piece begs a lot of obvious questions. Has he tackled the rampant antisemitism on college campuses across America? Is he writing editorials in *The New York Times* about that? Is he confronting radical college students who are harassing and abusing Jews on campus? Because if he is, I haven't seen the coverage. Instead, what he did was create a cheap shot at Bill Maher, presumably because he truly believes that Trump is Hitler.

Now, don't get me wrong—as I already wrote, Bill Maher is not getting any points from me. But what Larry David did is worse. He trivialized the death of millions of his own people simply to score some points against a comedic rival—and probably snag a few more backslaps at the next Beverly Hills wine-and-cheese party. It's pathetic.

Larry David knows better—or at least he should. You wouldn't see Jerry Seinfeld pulling that kind of bullshit, at least I don't think so. This isn't just about bad jokes; it reflects a broader trend of trivializing the Holocaust and the real horrors that came with it. It's a dangerous game to play when you start throwing around the name of Hitler as a punchline.

By doing so, David and others like him distract from the real fight against antisemitism and other forms of hatred that are, unfortunately, alive and well in today's society. Instead of using their platforms to challenge these issues, they choose to engage in cheap theatrics. It's easy to call Trump Hitler; it's much harder to confront the actual malignancy of hate and bigotry that persists in our society.

The irony is, while these "comedians" and political figures draw comparisons to Hitler, they miss the mark entirely. They fail to recognize that the real danger lies not in political disagreements but in the normalization of hatred and the trivialization of genocide. It's as if they're so caught up in their own narrative that they forget the historical context of the comparisons they're making.

When someone invokes Hitler, they're not just being hyperbolic—they're minimizing the suffering of millions who faced real horrors. They're cheapening the struggles of those who stand against real fascism, real oppression, and real injustice. And for what? A laugh? A trending topic on X? It's not just irresponsible; it's an abdication of the moral responsibility that comes with having a voice in today's society.

So, as we move forward, let's hold ourselves accountable for the language we use and the comparisons we make. Let's stop invoking Hitler as a crutch for our political arguments or as fodder for our comedic routines. If we truly care about the legacy of those who suffered under regimes like his, we need to treat that history with the seriousness it deserves.

Larry David and others like him may think they're being edgy or clever, but in reality, they're just part of a larger trend of trivialization that does nothing to advance constructive dialogue. So, let's aim higher. Let's engage in discussions that matter, that challenge us, and that respect the history we're all a part of. Because invoking Hitler isn't just a bad joke; it's a disservice to the memory of those who suffered, and a failure to address the pressing issues of our time.

◆ 27 ◆

THE WANING INFLUENCE OF CELEBRITY CULTURE IN POLITICS

YOU KNOW, THERE WAS A time when a celebrity could waltz into a political race and make it rain votes like they were throwing dollar bills at a strip club. I mean, think about it—back in the day, if you had a Hollywood star endorsing you, it was like having a magic wand. I'm talking about the days when a George Clooney or a Taylor Swift could carry a candidate straight to the White House. But here we are, and that's just not the case anymore. As I sit down to write this chapter, I realize this celebrity culture we've all been obsessed with is starting to fade faster than a Kardashian's marriage.

We live in a celebrity-obsessed culture, no doubt about it. It's like we've traded in our heroes for influencers. Gone are the days when actors were revered for their craft. Today's celebrity is more about how many followers you can rack up on TikTok than how many Oscars you've won. It's a whole new ball game, and let me tell you, it's not necessarily a good one.

Now, I'm not saying social media influencers don't have their place. They do—just not in the political arena. Sure, they can sell you a skincare routine or a diet plan, but when it comes to understanding what's going on in the heart of America? Let's just say I wouldn't trust a makeup guru to explain the intricacies of healthcare reform. The new wave of celebrity is more concerned with likes and shares than with the lives of everyday Americans. They've got the attention of millions, but when it comes time to actually make a difference? It's crickets.

Let's take a look back at the past presidential election, shall we? Remember when Joe Biden was running for a second term? Back in the day, you would have expected a full-court press from A-list celebrities. Taylor Swift would be singing her heart out at rallies, George Clooney would be hosting star-studded fundraisers, and everyone would be wearing matching "Biden 2020" T-shirts. But what happened? Well, it turns out that people have gotten wise. The influence celebrities once had is waning, and it's about time.

I mean, can you imagine the likes of Taylor Swift or Bette Midler trying to prop up Biden these days? The reality is, people are starting to see through the glitter. They're realizing that these celebrities, while talented, are often completely out of touch with the struggles of the average American. Celebrities are living in their mansions, while most are just trying to pay their bills and put food on the table. So, when Bette Midler starts ranting about the plight of the working class, you can bet people are rolling their eyes and thinking, "What does she know about it?"

And recall the political opinions of stars like Barbra Streisand and Jane Fonda. Sure, they've been around; they've had their time in the spotlight. But their opinions seem more rooted in their disdain for Donald Trump than any real understanding of the issues facing everyday people. It's like they've forgotten that not everyone can afford to live in a bubble of privilege. When they speak, it's not coming from a place of understanding but rather from a place of elitism. And people are catching on.

One of my favorite moments in the past election was watching the aftermath of celebrity endorsements. You know the drill: a famous actor tweets their support for a candidate, and the media goes wild. But then, the candidate loses, and suddenly the narrative shifts. "Oh, maybe celebrities don't have the influence we thought they did!" It's almost like a light bulb went off in the collective consciousness of America. People realized that just because you starred in a blockbuster doesn't mean you have the answers to our nation's problems.

I'm not saying I have a problem with celebrities wanting to get involved in politics. Go ahead, use your platform! But don't be shocked when Americans push back. Don't be surprised when your candidate gets obliterated, and yes, that might just mean Americans are sending a message about you as well. It's like the universe is saying, "We see you, and we're not buying what you're selling."

There's a difference between speaking out for a cause, and using your fame as a platform to push a political agenda. When celebrities start to think they're the voice of the people, that's when things get dicey. They may think they're helping, but most of us are just looking for someone who understands the grind of daily life—not another pampered star telling us how to vote based on the number of their Instagram followers.

Let's take a moment to appreciate the irony of it all. Here we are, living in a time when social media influencers have taken the stage; and yet, they can't seem to hold a candle to the political influence of past celebs. Remember when a celebrity endorsement meant something? Now, it's like a participation trophy. "Oh, you like my lipstick? Thanks for your vote!" Yeah, that's not how it works, honey.

And the beauty of this shift is that it's forcing politicians to actually engage with the issues that matter to real people. Instead of relying on celebrity endorsements to carry them over the finish line, candidates are being pushed to connect with their constituents on a more personal level. They're being forced to listen to the concerns of the average Joe rather than just relying on the glitz and glamour of Hollywood. This is a good thing. It means politicians are being held accountable.

I mean, celebrities aren't the ones who are going to pay your medical bills or secure your job, are they? They're not the ones who are going to be there when your kid needs help with their homework, or when you're trying to figure out how to get through another winter without heat. That's the reality of life for most Americans. And when celebrities come in like some kind of saviors, people are starting to see it for what it is—just another way to distract us from the real issues at hand.

So let's keep this in mind: the days of celebrities holding sway over politics are dwindling. People are waking up, and they're realizing that they need to rely on themselves rather than on the opinions of people who live in a completely different world. And that's a beautiful thing.

Look, I'm all for celebrities using their platforms to effect change. But let's not pretend that their influence is what it used to be. The American people are starting to see through the smoke and mirrors. They're recognizing that celebrity culture isn't the answer to our political problems. It's time for politicians to step up, engage with the real issues, and leave the celebrity endorsements in the past, where they belong. Because when all is said and done, it's not about who can tweet the best—it's about who can actually make a difference in people's lives. And that, my friends, is where the real power lies.

◆ 28 ◆

FACING MY DEMONS

I'VE ALWAYS HAD A COMPLICATED relationship with the gym. For years, I've been that guy who could show up, lift heavy, sweat buckets, and then go home without a second thought. But lately? Lately, I've felt a shift. It's like my mind has decided to show up and actually engage in the process, and it's a whole different ball game now.

People keep asking me, "What are you training for?" It feels like they expect a grand comeback or something. Sure, never say never when it comes to wrestling, but that's not the point right now. This is about something deeper—something more personal. I finally decided to confront the toughest opponent I've ever faced:

Myself.

For a long time, I was comfortable in my own skin, but that comfort often morphed into complacency. I let that little voice in my head—the one that whispers doubts, laziness, and the temptation to indulge in comfort food—take control. It was time to tell it to shut the hell up.

Food had become my biggest adversary. I realized that when I was having a rough day, my instinct was to reach for the nearest junk food. Acknowledging that was the first step. I had to look myself in the mirror and say, "You're not winning anymore. I am." The only way to do that was to dismantle the bad habits I had built over the years.

I'd drive past fast-food joints and think, "Not today, McDonald's." I made a conscious choice to break those habits that had been ingrained in me for decades. They say it takes two weeks to break a habit, but I'd been carrying this one around for thirty years. So, I knuckled down and faced it head-on.

When those cravings hit, I didn't let them fester. I spoke out loud to myself. I refused to keep my thoughts bottled up. It's astonishing how persuasive that little voice can be, convincing you that one burger won't hurt. But I learned to push through the discomfort, to do things that I didn't want to do.

Every time I hit that threshold in my mind where my brain was screaming, "Don't do it!" I just did the right thing anyway. I kept repeating a simple mantra: "Do the work." That's it. "Do the work." I started posting about it, hoping to inspire others who might be battling their own inner demons—the ones that tell you to be lazy, to indulge, to give up.

My son was also grappling with his weight. We decided to tackle this together. We got up early for our morning shakes, trained side by side, and documented our journey. What started as a six-week commitment turned into something much bigger—it became a lifestyle. I've always believed that first you form a habit, then it becomes a routine, and eventually, that routine becomes your religion. That's where I am now.

I can look myself in the eye and know exactly what I need to do. There's power in that clarity. It's easy to hate on others who are winning, but when you channel that energy inward, the results can be transformative.

As for my workouts? I'm training at Hard Knock South with some incredible coaches. My routine is built on solid principles: three sets of ten to twelve reps, or five, depending on the lift. I keep rest between sets to a minute or less—I want to keep my heart rate up. It's not about lifting the heaviest weights; it's about movement and consistency.

I mix it up: benching, squats, deadlifts, and plenty of cardio. I aim for four solid gym days a week and fill the rest with whatever I can find to keep moving. There are no excuses. If I'm not at the gym, I'm working out wherever I can, and I stick to a few simple rules.

I'll do five sets of five on squats and bench press, and then I add in what I call "burnouts" with resistance bands. I even started boxing on the heavy bag—first, I aimed for two minutes, then three, and now I'm hitting the bag for whole songs. Gradually, it all adds up.

I've also changed my diet. I'm on a regimen of shakes, thanks to my buddy Mike Bell, and I'm eating real food—steak and vegetables. Food is fuel, and I don't miss the junk. The happiest part of my day isn't about what's on my plate; it's realizing that I'm doing what I need to do to be there for my kids and myself.

But being in the gym is about more than just lifting weights; it's about lifting myself up. It's about proving to myself that I can face my demons and come out stronger on the other side. That's the real victory.

Now, I want you to think about your own life. What demons are you facing? What bad habits are holding you back? Maybe it's food, maybe it's procrastination, or perhaps it's something deeper that you haven't even acknowledged yet. The first step to overcoming those challenges is to confront them rather than hiding or making excuses for them. Look in the mirror and have that honest conversation with yourself.

Decide that you're not going to let those voices win anymore. Take action, even if it's small. Do the work, whatever that means for you. It's not easy, but it's worth it. When you focus on yourself and your own growth, you'll be amazed at what you can achieve.

Remember, you're not alone in this struggle. Everyone has their battles; it's part of being human. Whether it's dealing with self-doubt, unhealthy habits, or emotional challenges, the journey starts with you taking that first step. Don't be afraid to dig deep and explore what's holding you back.

Embrace the discomfort of change; it's a sign that you're growing. Surround yourself with people who inspire you, and don't underestimate the power of community. Share your journey with others. You might be surprised at how many people relate to your struggle and want to join you in the fight.

So, take a moment to reflect. What are you willing to change? What are you willing to fight for? Channel that energy, push through the barriers, and transform your life. The journey begins today. You have the strength within you; it's time to unleash it.

◆ 29 ◆

THE BIDEN PRESIDENCY:

A HISTORICAL SCANDAL

WHEN I LOOK BACK AT the Biden presidency, I don't hesitate to call it what it was: the greatest treasonous scandal in the history of our country. You heard me right. No other presidency has been as corrupt, fake, and dishonest as that one. It's almost laughable if it weren't so dangerous.

Here's the deal: Joe Biden, or as I prefer to call him, "the guy in the Oval Office," didn't even seem to understand the executive orders he signed. You know why? Because they just stuck a pen in his hand or let the auto-pen do the work. He'd never been in a meeting that wasn't scripted or controlled by someone else. It was like watching a bad movie where the lead actor couldn't remember his lines.

This guy needed note cards just to talk to friendly crowds. I'm not kidding. He's sitting at a dinner table with people cutting him checks for millions of dollars, and he's reading off a teleprompter to remember their names! That's not leadership; that's a puppet show. The whole time, the media, his co-conspirators in this farce, are telling us he's as sharp as a tack. If sharp means dull, then sure, let's go with that.

Now, let's consider his handlers, particularly his press secretary. Day after day, she would step up to that podium and spin a web of lies so thick you'd need a chainsaw to cut through it. "We can't even keep up with him!" they would say, as if Joe Biden was out there running marathons instead of stumbling through speeches. "He's never been stronger!" they insisted, while the reality was that he could barely string two sentences together without the help of a teleprompter. It was a masterclass in gaslighting, and it was all happening right in front of our eyes.

According to a recent report from *The New York Times*, Biden's inner circle was well aware of his age-related challenges. They were working overtime to manage how the public perceived him. Six key figures, including his wife Jill and son Hunter, were convinced he could and should run for a second term. Talk about a family that's got your back—right into the ground! But in all honesty, it's easy to cheerlead when your livelihood is tied to the guy in charge.

Longtime strategist Mike Donilon and counselor Steve Ricchetti were the gatekeepers of information, sometimes delaying bad polling numbers. You've got to hand it to them; they knew how to keep the ship afloat, even if it meant sailing through some very murky waters. Meanwhile, Annie Tomasini, Biden's deputy chief of staff, and Anthony Bernal, the first lady's top aide, were on a mission to keep Biden's schedule tight and the public perception even tighter. Their collective goal? Convince America that Biden was fit for another term, all while he was showing more signs of aging than a family sedan with a hundred thousand miles on it.

Three unnamed aides even overheard Donilon tell Biden in mid-2022, "Your biggest issue is the perception of age." And Biden was clearly showing signs that he was aging faster than a carton of milk left out on the kitchen counter. He was speaking more slowly than he had just a few years before, struggling to lift himself out of the presidential limousine. I mean, come on! The man looked like he was auditioning for a role in a retirement home drama. Some aides even thought he seemed disoriented at times, lost in a fog that made you wonder if he was looking for the nearest bingo hall instead of solutions for America's problems.

They had him using a teleprompter all the time—even for small fundraisers in donors' homes! Imagine that: you're at a swanky dinner party, and the president of the United States is reading from a screen like he's giving a high school speech. And what about the steps to Air Force One—they actually shortened them! I guess they figured that if Biden couldn't navigate those steps without a cane, he might as well have a little help from the flight crew.

At the same time, his team was scolding reporters for any coverage that dared to mention Biden's age-related challenges. They were out there convincing allies to write articles and social media posts pushing back against the negative press. It was like watching a bad episode of *Survivor*, where the tribe was determined to keep their leader in power no matter how many challenges he failed.

Now, let's pivot to the investigation into Biden's handling of classified documents. He managed to sidestep any criminal charges, but the political blowback from special counsel Robert Hur's report was even more devastating. The portrait painted of Biden was not one of a strong leader, but rather of a man who couldn't remember when he served as Barack Obama's vice president or the year his beloved son Beau died. That's a tough pill to swallow if you're trying to convince America that you're fit for another four years in the hot seat. The special counsel even noted that in a potential trial, Biden would likely come across as "a sympathetic, well-meaning, elderly man with a poor memory.". Talk about a perfect storm of negative perceptions.

All the while, Biden's own pride fueled a mission to prove his vitality. He was going to show the world that he was still the same man who had climbed the political ladder. But sometimes, those efforts backfired spectacularly. Remember when he broke his foot just before his inauguration? Instead of wearing an orthopedic boot to help him heal, he decided that would make him look weak. The result? That injury never healed correctly and left him shuffling around like a penguin with a hernia.

Now please, don't let anyone fool you into thinking this is just a sad chapter in history. This is a warning shot. The American people deserve better than a president who can't string a coherent thought together without a script. We've got to wake up and demand accountability, because if we don't, we're setting ourselves up for more disasters down the line.

And let's address that accountability issue for a moment. Why aren't more Democrats calling for transparency regarding the Biden presidency? Because they never cared about Joe Biden in the first place. He was nothing more than a tool to beat Donald Trump. Once that mission was accomplished, it was game over for Uncle Joe. His party threw him under the bus in the blink of an eye, and he probably barely realized what was happening. But you can bet your bottom dollar that they did. They care about power, not honesty or decency toward the country, or Biden himself.

Now, Republicans are far from perfect, but I can tell you this: they would never have pulled the kind of stunt that the Democrats pulled with Biden. This whole saga needs to be investigated, no matter how long it takes. We hear every day about how January 6 was the worst day in modern history; but let's take a good hard look at the worst presidency in modern history and get to the bottom of what really happened.

In the end, when historians look back at his presidency, they won't just see Joe Biden; they'll see a whole circus of mismanagement and deception. As for us, we've gotten a warning that letting incompetence take the wheel can lead to treachery at the highest level. And believe me, we can't afford to ignore that lesson. The Biden presidency is more than just a chapter in history; it's a cautionary tale for the future. Let's make sure we learn from it.

◆ 30 ◆

INSANE NEWS:
THE MEDIA'S ENDLESS LOOP OF LUNACY

THEY SAY THE DEFINITION OF insanity is doing the same thing over and over and expecting a different outcome. If that's the case, then the mainstream media is the poster child for insanity. As I sit here writing this, it's become painfully clear that they've learned absolutely nothing from the last time Donald Trump was in office. It's the same petty games, the same intolerant attitudes, and the same kind of advocacy that made them look foolish the first time around. It's as if they've hit the repeat button on a broken record, and quite frankly, I'm getting tired of hearing the same old tune.

Once again, we're treated to a relentless barrage of headlines about "threats to democracy" and other buzzwords that have become so overused they hardly warrant a click anymore. Watching the media is like watching a toddler throw a tantrum because they can't have a cookie—angry, petulant, and utterly out of touch with reality. The media have been dying a slow death for years; yet here they are, clinging desperately to whatever relevance they may still have. And what do they do with that waning significance? They target Trump with whatever's left in the chamber...metaphorically speaking, of course.

Don't forget the first attempt on Trump's political life came not from some shadowy figure lurking in the night, but from the mainstream media. Fueled by cynicism and an insatiable thirst for scandal, they've turned journalism into a carnival act. The headlines are just clickbait and the facts take a backseat to outrage. I'm not saying they had to be heartbroken over the last election, but a little objectivity wouldn't hurt. Instead, they've doubled down on their biases, concocting narratives to fit their agendas and ignoring the general mood of the country.

By the time you're holding this book, I'm sure the ratings for major networks will have dropped a few more points. It's a trend we've been watching for years. Meanwhile, here at Fox News, we're doing just fine, thank you very much. The gap between what the mainstream media deliver and what people actually want to consume is widening, and it's no wonder why. The press has dug itself into a hole so deep that it's practically a bottomless pit. They've become so obsessed with attacking and maligning the president that they've lost sight of their purpose: to inform the public, not to spin tales of doom and gloom based on personal politics.

Now, many journalists love to say that the purpose of the media is to "afflict the comfortable and comfort the afflicted." What a bunch of bullshit. First of all, what happens when you comfort the afflicted to the point that they then *become* the comfortable? Do you just switch gears and go after them next? It's a never-ending cycle of victimhood and resentment, and it's why that cliché is such crap. Hey, Mr. Reporter: you are not in business to comfort anybody or afflict anybody. When did that become part of journalism? Your job is to accurately report what is happening, even when it clashes with your prejudices or hurts your fragile ego.

Think about it. If the media were truly committed to afflicting the comfortable, then they'd be taking a hard look at the powerful elites pulling the strings—the politicians who are supposed to serve the people but are more concerned with their own careers and image. Instead, they focus their energy on sensational stories that generate clicks and views, often at the expense of nuanced reporting. It's like they're too scared to challenge the status quo, so they stick to the safe narrative that fits their agenda...which is attention-seeking and ad-generating.

This isn't just about Trump, either. It's about a media that's lost its core purpose and credibility. The same outlets that claimed to be the guardians of truth have become the harbingers of hysteria. They've traded in investigative journalism for lurid headlines, and the result is a populace that's more confused than informed. When the media are more interested in clicks than in context, you end up with a society that's divided, angry, and misinformed.

Take the recent coverage of Trump's legal challenges. Instead of presenting the facts and letting the audience draw their own conclusions, the media have opted for a narrative that paints Trump as a villain in a never-ending saga. They're not reporting; they're actively generating a *story* that fits their preconceived notions. And in doing so, they've lost the trust of a significant portion of the American public. It's no wonder that people are turning to alternative sources for their news—

sources that might not always be perfect but at least offer a different perspective.

What's truly baffling is that the mainstream media seem to think this approach is sustainable. They're like a chef who keeps serving the same burnt dish, expecting old customers to return just because it's been on the menu forever. They've ignored the fact that the world has changed. The old ways of doing things no longer resonate with an audience hungry for honesty and authenticity. Instead, they've doubled down on the same tired tropes, convinced that their audience will come back for more.

So, what's the solution? It's simple: the media need to realize that their credibility is hanging by a thread. So, instead of indulging in hyperbole and hysteria, they should focus on delivering accurate, balanced reporting that reflects the diverse views of the American people. They need to get back to the basics of journalism—investigate, inform, and inspire. But that's a tall order when they've become so entrenched in their own biases.

And please recall the role of social media in all of this. Platforms like X and Substack have given rise to a new kind of citizen journalism, where anyone with a smartphone can share their perspective. While this has its drawbacks—hello, misinformation!—social media also is a powerful tool for amplifying voices that have been marginalized by traditional media. People are tired of the same narrative being pushed by the mainstream outlets, and they're seeking out alternatives. The old guard is scrambling to keep up, but instead of adapting, they're digging in their heels and doubling down on their failed strategies.

It's a losing battle, and they know it. Their ratings are in free fall, and their audiences are slipping away like water through their fingers. They've tried every gimmick to regain their footing—outrage, sensationalism, and fearmongering—but none of it has worked. People are smarter than they give credit for, and they're not willing to put up with the same old song and dance anymore.

If the media truly want to regain the trust of the American people, they need to take a long, hard look in the mirror. They need to stop playing the blame game and start taking responsibility for their role in the current state of affairs. They need to recognize that their obsession with Trump isn't just a matter of politics; it's a reflection of their own insecurities and biases. They've painted themselves into a corner, and the only way out is to acknowledge their mistakes and make a concerted effort to change.

The media have the power to shape public discourse, but with great power comes great responsibility. It's time for them to remember that their job is to inform, not inflame. They need to stop treating every news cycle like it's the end of the world and start focusing on the stories that matter to the American people. The country is facing real challenges—economic struggles, social unrest, and a growing sense of division—and the media have a duty to cover these issues with the seriousness they deserve.

But will they? Only time will tell. As it stands, they seem more interested in clinging to their fading relevance than in serving the public interest. The longer they continue down this path of insanity, the more they'll lose sight of their purpose and the more they'll alienate their audiences. It's time for the media to step back from the brink and remember what it means to be a journalist. If they can't do that, then they might as well hand over their office keys to the next generation of reporters who are ready to do the job right.

In the end, the choice is theirs. They can continue to spiral into irrelevance, or they can rise to the occasion and reclaim their place as trusted sources of information. But until they do, the rest of us will be tuning out, shaking our heads at the insanity of it all. Because in a world where the news has become nothing more than a circus sideshow, it's hard to take it seriously—especially when the clowns are the ones holding the microphone. And we've had enough of the clown show.

◆ 31 ◆

THE GREAT CLIMATE CHANGE CIRCUS

REMEMBER WHEN BIDEN TOOK OFFICE and his favorite phrase was "the greatest existential crisis facing mankind"? He practically wore it on a T-shirt. It was all "climate change this" and "climate change that." You couldn't turn on the news without hearing him and his pals conjure up visions of the apocalypse, like it was a bad horror movie. But now? Crickets. The Democrats have suddenly decided that climate change is as relevant as my grandma's old VHS tapes.

Why? Because it was all a ploy. A political tool to get their foot in the door and push their agenda. The moment Trump took office a second time, it was like someone flipped a switch. The urgency disappeared faster than a cheeseburger at a barbecue. If climate change was such a dire issue, why aren't these left-wing warriors out in the streets with their picket signs and protest chants? I'll tell you why: because nobody bought their BS.

I mean, look at the poster children for this hypocrisy: AOC and Bernie Sanders. These two are flying around the country in private jets like they're on a luxury tour of the world. If they really cared about climate change, wouldn't they be taking a bus, or heck, even a bicycle? But no, that would require some actual sacrifice, and we all know they're not about that kind of life. Instead, they're sipping lattes and pinot grigio while jetting off to conferences in exotic locales, all while preaching to you about saving the planet. Talk about a carbon footprint! Maybe they think the rules don't apply to them because they've got a "D" next to their names.

And remember Al Gore? This guy has been crying wolf about climate change since before most of us even knew what a "climate" was. His predictions have been about as safe as a blindfolded squirrel trying to cross the road. Remember when he said that the polar ice caps would be gone by now? Yeah, they're still there, hanging around like the last kid picked for dodgeball. Nature has a funny way of turning the tables on these doomsday prophets. Every time they predict the end of the world, nature gives them a big ol' middle finger and keeps on trucking.

The truth is, climate change is just another left-wing scam. If it really were the crisis they claim it to be, they'd be out there fighting tooth and nail, just like they were during the Biden administration. But now? It's like they've suddenly realized that maybe, just maybe, it's not as big of a deal as they made it out to be. They've moved on to the next social justice trend, some new shiny object to distract us with. Hey, look over there, everybody! See our latest manufactured outrage!

Let's break down the "solutions" these Democrats keep throwing at us. Every time they come up with a new plan, it's not about saving the environment; it's about lining the pockets of lobbyists and their wealthy benefactors. They'll throw out phrases like "green energy" and "sustainable practices" while they're secretly cashing checks from the very industries they claim to be fighting against. It's like a magician performing a trick right in front of you, and you're just supposed to sit there and clap like a seal.

Take a look at all those climate conferences they love to hold in far-off, exotic places. You know, the ones that require a small army of private jets to attend? If these activists really cared about the planet, wouldn't they be using Zoom? I mean, we all figured it out during the pandemic, right? But no, they'd rather hop on a fleet of jets and spew out enough carbon to choke a continent. Gee, it's almost like they think they're above the rules they set for the rest of us, isn't it?

Every time they gather in these lavish locations, it's like they're throwing a party...with a side of climate guilt. "Look at us! We're saving the world!" they shout, while the rest of us are just trying to figure out how to keep our own lights on. The irony is thicker than the smog in Los Angeles. Meanwhile, I'm over here wondering how they don't see the hypocrisy in their actions. They're preaching about saving the planet while simultaneously contributing to its downfall.

And let's take a closer look at the environmental policies they propose. It's as if they're taking scientific and economic advice from a toddler who just discovered crayons. They come up with these grand plans that sound great on paper but have absolutely no connection to reality. They want us to believe that switching to electric cars is the answer, but have they ever thought about where the electricity to charge their batteries comes from? It's not from magic! No, those power plants spewing smoke and generating electricity aren't going anywhere anytime soon.

Then there's the whole renewable energy debate. Sure, wind and solar sound nice, but have you ever seen a solar panel farm? It's like a graveyard of shiny rectangles that do nothing but take up space and kill the local wildlife. And please don't get me started on the environmental impact of mining for the minerals needed for those batteries. It's a vicious cycle, and they're too busy patting themselves on the back to notice.

Now, let's focus on the messaging. These climate warriors have mastered the art of scaring people into compliance. They throw around phrases like "the planet is on fire" and "we're all going to die" as if they're trying to win an Oscar for Best Dramatic Performance. They'd have you believe that if you don't recycle your soda cans and switch to biodegradable straws, you're personally responsible for polar bears drowning in the Arctic. Give me a break!

The truth is, they're playing on our emotions. They want us to feel guilty, to feel small, to feel like we need to bow down to their "superior" knowledge. But nature has a funny way of working itself out. Yes, we should be responsible stewards of the planet, but it doesn't mean we need to live in a constant state of fear. The weather is always going to be changing. Surprise! It's called nature, idiots. It's been happening long before any of us were around, and it'll keep happening long after we're gone. The climate has always gone through cycles—hot, cold, wet, dry. That's the way it is. It's not some grand conspiracy or a sign of the apocalypse. It's just Mother Nature doing her thing. But instead of accepting that, these climate warriors want to put the blame on us, the average folks just trying to make a living.

So, no—climate change is not the greatest existential crisis facing mankind. It's just another political scam used to push an agenda and line the pockets of the elite. If it were as important as they claim, they'd be out there fighting for it instead of enjoying their private jets and indulging their luxurious lifestyles.

So, the next time you hear a politician or activist raving about climate change, remember: it's just another act in their political carnival. The real crisis? That's the one where we have to protect ourselves from left-wing sideshow shysters trying to sell us a bill of goods.

It's about time we start calling out these charlatans for what they are. The fate of the planet shouldn't rest on the shoulders of those who are more interested in padding their bank accounts than actually making a difference. Instead, let's rise above their noise, laugh at the absurdity of it all, and remember: nature is going to do what nature does.

And if they keep flying high on their private jets while preaching sustainability, we'll be here, feet planted firmly on the ground, keeping it real and calling out their hypocrisy. Because the only existential crisis we should be focused on is figuring out how to sift through the BS and find the truth. And that is a crisis worth tackling.

◆ 32 ◆

A MORAL CODE FOR THE MODERN AGE:

FINDING OUR WAY BACK

I'M NOT A RELIGIOUS GUY. I don't go to church, I don't subscribe to a specific belief system, and I definitely don't believe in paying someone to be my spiritual middleman. But even as a non-religious person, I can't shake the feeling that we need to get back to a moral code in this country. Somewhere along the line, we've lost our way, and it's time to talk about it—no holds barred.

Now, I know what you're thinking: "Tyrus, how can you advocate for a moral code when you don't even believe in organized religion?" Well, let me tell you something. Just because I don't believe in the church doesn't mean I don't see the value in the principles that have shaped our society. Take the Ten Commandments, for instance. You can call yourself an atheist all you want, but if you grew up in a Christian society, those rules are ingrained in you. They're like the operating manual for life in America. You can say you don't believe in God, but if you think that gives you a free pass to go around killing people, you've got another think coming.

I mean, come on! The moral framework we live by was built on these foundational principles, and for good reason. They provide a structure, a guideline for how to treat one another, whether you're a believer or not. So while I'm not signing up for Sunday services anytime soon, I can appreciate that these moral codes exist for a reason. They help keep society from spiraling into chaos.

Now, don't get me wrong. I'm skeptical of organized religion. I think it's a hustle in many ways. You've got people out there paying for their connection to God, and honestly, that's just a con. Why on Earth do I need to go through some guy in a robe with a fancy title to get to the big guy upstairs? If you need a middleman to reach your creator, that sounds like a scam to me!

Take a look at some of these religious leaders. You ever notice how many of them are living large? You've got preachers with Rolexes on their wrists and private jets in their hangars. Hold up! If Jesus was a carpenter, how did his alleged spokesmen end up in mansions while his followers are struggling to make rent? I mean, the man was humble, and yet here we are, watching "men of God" roll in luxury cars. That's not faith; that's a business model!

My issue with organized religion goes deeper than just the flashy lifestyles. I've been curious about this stuff for a long time. I didn't just wake up one day and decide I didn't like church. No, I studied it. I experimented. I took the time to understand what's out there. I even dabbled in some religions during college, looking for answers. I sat through Catholic mass, and I participated in Ramadan with a buddy of mine whose dad had really high expectations for him—naming him

"Messiah" was a bold move, to say the least. I mean, no pressure there, right?

What I found was a mixed bag. There's a lot of good in the teachings, but there's also a lot of hypocrisy. So many people preach one thing and then turn around and act completely differently. They'll tell you how to live your life while they're busy living in a way that contradicts those very principles. That's the kind of stuff that makes me roll my eyes and question everything.

But just because I'm skeptical of organized religion doesn't mean I'm against the idea of having a moral compass. In fact, I believe it's more important than ever to establish one. We are living in a time when moral relativism runs rampant. People seem to have lost sight of right and wrong, and that's a dangerous road to travel.

We need to get back to a place where we can agree on some fundamental values. I'm talking about respect, honesty, integrity, and responsibility. These aren't just nice words to throw around; they should be the foundation of our society. We need to start holding ourselves and each other accountable. It's not enough to just say, "I'm a good person." We need to demonstrate it through our actions.

In this world of social media and instant gratification, it's all too easy to get lost in the noise. People are more focused on likes and retweets than they are on making a genuine impact. It's about time we cut through the BS and get back to what really matters. We need to stop being so consumed by our own interests and start thinking about the greater good.

Let's consider the reality of our times. We're living in a society that seems to reward selfishness and ego over empathy and cooperation. Look at the headlines! We see politicians caught in scandals, public figures behaving badly, and a general atmosphere of distrust. It's like we're in a moral free-for-all, and that's not okay. We need to reclaim our values, not just for ourselves but for the future generations who will inherit this mess.

I'm not saying we need to return to some rigid, dogmatic system. What I'm advocating for is a return to fundamental human decency. We need to foster a culture that values kindness, honesty, and accountability. We need to teach our children that actions have consequences and that integrity matters.

Let's break it down further. You know how we have rules in sports? You can't just run onto the field and do whatever you want. There are referees, rules, and consequences for breaking them. Why don't we have the same kind of accountability in our everyday lives? If you do something wrong, there should be a price to pay. It's that simple.

Some will say, "Tyrus, who are you to talk about morality?" Fair point. But having a moral compass isn't about being religious; it's about being a decent human being. And let's be honest, we're all a little lost right now. It's time we start navigating in the right direction.

One of the biggest challenges we face is that the people in power often don't live by the same moral code they expect from the rest of us. They make decisions that benefit themselves while ignoring the needs of their constituents. We see politicians who want to preach about social justice while their own lives don't reflect those values. That hypocrisy erodes trust and makes it difficult for people to believe in anything.

It's also worth noting that a lot of this moral decay is rooted in the absence of accountability. If people don't fear the consequences of their actions, they're less likely to act responsibly. So how do we change that? We need to start holding each other accountable. If someone is acting out of line, call them out on it! If you see someone doing wrong, don't just stand by and watch. Stand up and say something.

In the end, it's about building a community that prioritizes morals over money. We can't let the pursuit of wealth overshadow our commitment to doing what's right. Imagine if we channeled even a fraction of that energy into helping one another. We could create a movement that actually makes a difference!

I get it. It's easy to throw your hands up and say, "What can I do?" But the truth is, it starts with each of us. Every small action has the potential to create a ripple effect. We need to raise the bar, not just for ourselves but for everyone around us. It's time to stop accepting mediocrity and start striving for something greater.

And there's the cultural aspect of this. We're living in a time where moral ambiguity is celebrated in popular culture. Just flip on the TV or scroll through social media, and you'll see it: reality shows glorifying bad behavior, music that promotes violence and disrespect, and a general sense that anything goes. This is the message our kids are absorbing, and it's troubling. We need to counteract that with positive role models and narratives that promote integrity and hard work.

We need to create an environment where people feel empowered to speak up. If someone is acting out of line, don't just ignore it. Step in and say, "Hey, that's not right." We've got to create a culture that values integrity over convenience.

You know, I've always believed that the fabric of our society is woven together by the values we hold dear. We need to start prioritizing those values again. It's not enough to just say we care; we have to show it. We have to be proactive in our pursuit of a better future, not just for ourselves but for the generations that will come after us.

Let's look at how this applies in our everyday lives. You don't have to be a politician to make a difference. In your community, at your job, in your family, you have the power to set an example. Stand up for what you believe in. Call out injustice when you see it. Be the person who encourages others to do the right thing. It may not be easy, but it's necessary.

Here's the challenge: let's reclaim our moral code. Let's start holding ourselves accountable and demand the same from those in power. It's time to get back to basics and remind ourselves what it means to be good human beings.

Yes, I might not be a religious man, but that doesn't mean I can't recognize the importance of a solid moral foundation. We can build the future we want to see, but it requires effort, integrity, and a commitment to doing what's right. So, let's get to work and make it happen! The future of our country depends on it.

And just remember: it doesn't take a divine revelation to know right from wrong. Sometimes, it just takes a little common sense and a willingness to stand up for what you believe in. That's the moral code we need to embrace. It's time to put aside our differences, our grudges, and our petty grievances, and come together as a community.

◆ 33 ◆

THE STUPIDITY OF STUPID DEMOCRATS

AS I TRAVEL AROUND THE country, one thing keeps popping up in the conversations I have with people: they're tired of being treated by the Democrats like they're stupid. It's almost laughable, yet incredibly frustrating how the left continues to operate under the delusion that they know better than the average American.

Let me tell you—the Democrats have made a habit of looking down their noses at the people they claim to represent. It's like they think they're the intellectual elite, while the rest of us are just a bunch of knuckle-dragging Neanderthals who can't possibly grasp the complexities of political discourse.

This attitude is the hallmark of the Democratic Party: "You're just too stupid to understand." They throw around this idea that if you disagree with them, it's not because you have a different perspective; it's because you simply lack the mental capacity to comprehend their brilliance. It's insulting, and Americans are over it. After losing to Trump—not once, but twice—you would think the Democrats might have learned a lesson about underestimating the intelligence of the electorate. But no, they continue to dig their own grave.

Any fair review of the polling and sentiments across this great nation reveals that a bipartisan consensus of people couldn't wait for Biden to leave office. Yet, you flicked on the television, and people onscreen, wearing their best serious faces, insisted how amazing this guy was. "Joe Biden is one of the greatest presidents! He's George Washington!" they said, and you couldn't help but shake your head.

The Democrats are still operating under the delusion that they can keep selling these sorts of phony narratives, that they can keep up the façade that everything under the Biden administration went just fine. But as far as their credibility is concerned, they are digging their own hole deeper and deeper, long after they've lost the election. It's the number one rule of being in a hole: Stop digging! Yet, they keep shoveling like they're in some sort of bizarre political competition to see who can bury themselves the fastest.

Take, for instance, the Senate Armed Services Committee hearing involving the nomination of Pete Hegseth for Secretary of Defense. If you tuned in, you saw what I saw: a relentless grilling about his personal life—his sexual history, his drinking habits—while the critical issues regarding national security strategy were pushed aside. Seriously, what would have benefited the American people more? Hearing about national security, or hearing about who Hegseth has been with? According to some Democrats, the latter is clearly more important. It's a classic case of misdirection—look over here, while the real issues are hanging out in the shadows.

Senator Tim Kaine, for instance, seemed more interested in digging into Hegseth's personal life than addressing the pressing issues facing our nation. His line of questioning was not just inappropriate; it was downright ridiculous. The

Democrats' theatrics during that hearing were so over the top that it was bound to backfire. They thought they were going to score political points by going for the jugular, but all they did was solidify Hegseth's nomination. Even some Republicans who were previously lukewarm about Hegseth pledged their support, and you can bet it's because of the Democrats' reckless behavior during that hearing. It's as if they didn't realize that the American people didn't vote for business as usual—they voted for a shakeup.

And what about this "TV stigma" that Democrats seem to have? Just because someone had a job at Fox News, they assume that person must be vapid and lacking in substance. But Hegseth wasn't just a pretty face on a TV screen; he's a military veteran with two decades of service and an Ivy League education. The guy has credentials! But all they saw was the surface, and they couldn't seem to look past their own biases.

This same condescending mindset permeates the Democratic Party as a whole. They genuinely believe they can dictate what the American people should think, feel, and believe. And when the public doesn't fall in line, they resort to name-calling and character attacks instead of engaging in meaningful dialogue. But they're the ones who are truly out of touch.

If they ever want to regain the trust of the people, the Democrats need to stop treating the American public like they're stupid. They need to realize that people are more informed than they give them credit for. The more the Democrats push this narrative that they're the enlightened ones, the more they alienate themselves from the very people they claim to represent.

As I travel from state to state, meeting people who are tired of being condescended to, I hear their frustrations loud and clear. They're fed up with the way the left continues to gaslight them. There's a palpable sense of anger among voters who feel that their intelligence is being insulted day in and day out. And guess what? They're not just going to take it lying down anymore.

The Democrats may think they can keep playing this game, but let me assure you, it's a losing strategy. And it's left them in a precarious position. They've alienated a significant portion of the electorate. The American people are smarter than they realize, and they're ready to push back. And as the midterms and future elections approach, they need to ask themselves if they can keep up this charade—or self-delusion—about their own supposed superiority. Because if the Democrats continue to treat voters like they're too stupid to understand the complexities of governance, then perhaps "stupid" isn't the right label for them to apply to others; it's the very definition of what it means to be a Democrat in today's political landscape.

The American people are demanding better treatment. They're tired of the condescension, and the outright stupidity that has become synonymous with the Democratic Party. It's time for the Democrats to realize that the era of treating voters like they're too ignorant to understand is over.

So here's my challenge to them: start engaging with the American people as equals. Stop assuming that you're the only ones with the answers. This isn't just about winning elections; it's about serving the people. If you want to regain some semblance of credibility, you need to start treating Americans with the respect they deserve. Otherwise, you're just going to keep digging that hole deeper. And the fed-up American public is ready to hand you the shovel.

◆ 34 ◆

LADY MACBIDEN:
A CALL FOR ACCOUNTABILITY

IN THE THEATER OF AMERICAN politics, few figures on the stage were as perplexing as Jill Biden—the former First Lady who somehow managed to transform her role into a blend of Miss America and Lady Macbeth. Yes, you heard that right: Lady MacBiden—a name that perfectly captures the blend of ambition and moral ambiguity that characterized her time in office.

Jill Biden was no innocent bystander in this political drama. Sure, she had the credentials: a long career as an educator, a doctorate in education, and a soft spot for children and families. But she was also married to the president of the United States, and that role came with a certain amount of responsibility. Instead of embracing transparency and accountability, she opted for a playbook that might have been titled *How to Control the Narrative*.

While it was easy to blame the staff for the messy decisions and cringe-worthy soundbites coming out of the White House, remember who was ultimately responsible. Yes, Joe

Biden's team might have been the ones pulling the strings, but it was Jill who stood right there, wearing a smile and waving the banner while the chaos unfolded. The press access restrictions? The carefully curated public persona? That was all her handiwork. If anyone thought she was just there to support her husband, they should think again. She was the gatekeeper, and it is time to take a closer look at what was behind that gate.

First, let's focus on Anthony Bernal, Jill's so-called "work husband." This guy was accused of bullying and verbally sexually harassing colleagues for more than a decade, yet he was considered "untouchable" because Jill Biden had his back.

Sources reported that Bernal, who wielded enormous clout as the First Lady's top aide, made crude comments about genitalia and sexuality with alarming frequency. What was particularly striking was that he had a theory—yes, a theory—that the size of a person's thumb corresponded to that of their genitalia. I couldn't even make this stuff up! What was next? A deep dive into the correlation between shoe size and intelligence? This wasn't just inappropriate; it was a classic case of "Me Too" waiting to happen.

Colleagues recounted his inappropriate remarks, including jabs about penis size, during workplace disagreements and comments about others' attractiveness, at the most awkward of moments. Really? Here you have a top Biden White House official who speculated about the penis sizes of his colleagues and made inappropriate remarks about their sexualities. This was the kind of behavior you'd expect from a middle-school locker room, not the halls of power in Washington, DC. In a world that had finally started to take sexual harassment seriously, how was it that this guy was still running around the White House like he owned the place?

Because Jill Biden, in her quest to control the narrative, allowed this culture to fester. By surrounding herself with such bullies and enabling their behavior, she didn't just fail to uphold the values of integrity and decency she so often espoused; she actively undermined them. "They talked a big game about integrity, decency, and kindness," one former adviser remarked, "but when you worked for the Bidens, you experienced anything but that."

So, here's the million-dollar question: should Jill Biden be held accountable? Because she wasn't just sitting in the background, knitting and smiling while her husband took the heat. She was complicit in the toxic culture that developed within her own office. By ignoring the troubling behavior of her closest aide, she didn't merely turn a blind eye; she endorsed it.

Lady MacBiden may have had a charming smile and a heartwarming story, but don't let that fool you. She was in this game for keeps, and while she was still First Lady, she should have faced the music. The American people deserved nothing less than accountability, but unfortunately, that had been lost in the pages of her carefully constructed narrative.

In the end, the fallout from Jill Biden's time in the White House should serve as a cautionary tale. It's a reminder that no one is above reproach, regardless of their title or the narrative they wish to project. Power can corrupt, and it often does, especially when the gatekeepers allow it to flourish unchecked. The very policies and values that the Bidens claimed to uphold were often overshadowed by the very behaviors they professed to oppose.

The hypocrisy was palpable. While they preached kindness and integrity, the inner workings of the White House told a different story. It was a place where bullying was tolerated, where inappropriate remarks flew under the radar, and where accountability was a foreign concept. For those who worked tirelessly in the trenches, the disconnect between the Bidens' public persona and the reality of their administration was not just disappointing; it was infuriating.

As we move forward, let's hope that the next First Lady—or any public figure, for that matter—learns from these missteps. Holding power accountable should not just be a tagline; it should be a mandate. And for Jill Biden, the echoes of her tenure will linger, a constant reminder that the price of ambition is often paid in lost integrity and shattered trust. The American people deserve leaders who not only speak of change but embody it in every action, and it's time for Lady MacBiden to reflect on the tarnished legacy she left behind.

◆ 35 ◆

CALIFORNIA DREAMIN':

MORE LIKE CALIFORNIA SCREAMIN'

AH, CALIFORNIA. THE LAND OF sunshine, palm trees, and the occasional celebrity meltdown. Growing up in the Golden State was like living in a postcard—if the postcard had a few wildfires, a sprinkle of homelessness, and a healthy dose of political madness. I've met plenty of folks who spent their formative years in California, soaking up the rays while trying to navigate the chaos. And you know what? They loved it. California was vibrant, alive, and as colorful as the graffiti on the walls of any San Francisco underpass.

But boy, how things have changed.

These days, California seems to be competing for the title of "Worst Place on Earth." And no, I'm not talking about the climate—sure, we've got some heat waves and wildfires, but that's not what's really burning us down. The real inferno comes from the high crime rates, the skyrocketing taxes, and the homeless population that's turning once-beautiful streets into a third-world country. It's like we're living in a dystopian novel, except the author forgot to include a coherent plot.

Let's start with crime. California's got crime rates that would make a New York City mugger envious. A short stroll through downtown LA can feel like a scene from *Mad Max*—minus the cool vehicles and futuristic fashion. People I know who still live there have told me it can feel like a game of Frogger just trying to cross the street without stepping on a drug deal or dodging a group of vagrants.

Next, consider the taxes. I'm pretty sure Californians are paying more in taxes than most countries have in GDP. And what about the high housing costs? Just look at what it costs to get a decent two-bedroom in San Francisco. You could buy a mansion in Texas for what you'd spend on a shoebox in the Bay Area.

Speaking of high costs, let's talk about the college scene. Back in the day, California was home to some of the best educational institutions in the nation. Now? The universities have turned into glorified party zones fueled by legalized pot. Sure, students are having a great time, but what's the point of getting a degree when you can't even afford to live in the state after graduation? It's like they're handing out diplomas with one hand and slapping on crippling student debt with the other.

Then there's the homelessness crisis. You can't walk five feet in San Francisco without tripping over a pop-up tent or stepping in something that definitely doesn't smell like roses. Friends who still live there tell me it's like living in a reality show where the producers forgot to pay the actors. The streets are littered with garbage and drug paraphernalia, and the local government seems more concerned with hiding the problem than actually solving it. At this point, California looks less like a paradise and more like an audition tape for a *Survivor* reboot.

Or take their illustrious Governor Gavin Newsom—please. This guy has painted California as the epicenter of progress, claiming it's "under attack" by conservatives and "delusional bashers." Newsom's got a real knack for gaslighting—he's out there telling everyone that California is leading the nation's economic growth, while the rest of us are watching our wallets shrink faster than our hairlines at a middle-school reunion. How does he reconcile that California is home to a third of the nation's welfare recipients while simultaneously claiming to be the world's fifth-largest economy? It's like saying you're a great chef while serving up a bowl of instant ramen and calling it gourmet.

Newsom's policies are so left-leaning that they might as well be on a permanent tilt. He's signed bills that allow public schools to keep parents in the dark about their kids' gender transitions. This "Support Academic Futures and Educators for Today's Youth Act" might be retitled the "Let's Replace Parents with School Counselors Act." It's pure Orwellian madness. Parents are left to wonder if their kid is learning algebra, or how to choose the best hormone therapy.

And while Newsom is busy signing bills that infringe on parental rights, the education system is crumbling faster than a sandcastle at high tide. People I know in California tell me the public schools are focused on teaching kids about 104 different genders instead of, you know, actual subjects like math or history. It's like they're trying to create a generation of "peak stupid" while ignoring the basics. At this rate, high school graduates will be woefully unprepared for the real world, but hey, they'll know all about gender theory.

Or how about the minimum wage debacle? Newsom's twenty-dollar fast-food minimum wage has led to thousands of job losses in an industry that traditionally serves as a stepping stone for young workers. Business owners are closing up shop or moving their operations out of state faster than you can say "taxes." But what does Newsom care? He's too busy patting himself on the back for all the "progress" he's making while his constituents are left scrambling for jobs.

And accountability? Forget about it. Newsom vetoed a bill that would have provided transparency on the state's homeless spending. Why? Because he'd rather keep the public in the dark about where their tax dollars are going. It's like he's playing a game of political hide-and-seek, but the only ones hiding are the people who should be held accountable.

Meanwhile, Californians are paying through the nose for insurance—homeowners, commercial properties, you name it. The rates are going up like an Elon Musk rocket, and for what? I've heard stories from friends who've moved out of state, and they can barely contain their laughter when they compare their insurance bills.

But hey, at least they have the weather, right? Oh wait, that's not even a sure thing anymore, with the droughts and water rationing. The state is in such a mess that it's almost comical. You'd think we'd be able to figure out how to manage water in a state that's essentially a giant desert, but there they are, rationing while the politicians are busy playing musical chairs with their policies.

In the end, California needs to get it together. It was once the land of opportunity and dreams, but now it's a cautionary tale. The people I know who still live there are frustrated, confused, and downright angry. They want to see change, but the left-wing political establishment is so entrenched that fighting it feels like trying to swim upstream in a river of quicksand.

So, here's to the California of my youth: the sun-soaked beaches, the eclectic people, and the wild adventures. Now? Now it's a state in chaos, sinking beneath the weight of its own absurdity. If only the folks in charge would take off their rose-colored glasses and see the mess they've made.

◆ 36 ◆

JUDGES GONE WILD

WE'VE GOT FEDERAL JUDGES ACTING like they're auditioning for a role in a bad courtroom drama, and it's about time someone called them out. The Justice Department just dropped the hammer on two judges—yes, you heard that right—two judges who decided to play fast and loose with the law, charged with allegedly obstructing federal law enforcement operations and helping illegal immigrants dodge the law.

First up on the chopping block is Milwaukee County Circuit Court Judge Hannah Dugan. Now, this judge thought it was her prerogative to turn the courthouse into a sanctuary for illegal immigrants. When US Immigration and Customs Enforcement (ICE) showed up to arrest a Mexican national named Eduardo Flores-Ruiz—who had already been deported and was back in the country illegally—Dugan decided to flex her judicial muscles.

According to reports, when Judge Dugan learned that ICE agents were in the courthouse waiting to arrest Flores-Ruiz, she didn't just sit back and let the law take its course. No, she confronted the agents and ordered them to leave. She told them they needed a judicial warrant, making it clear she was more interested in protecting a criminal than upholding the law. And then, Dugan decided she could whisk him out the back door, like a magician pulling a rabbit out of a hat.

Really, Judge Dugan? You think you're the gatekeeper, now? That's not how this works!

Let's break this down: Dugan was supposed to ensure justice, not obstruct it. When federal agents arrive with a lawful arrest warrant, the last thing you do is act like a bouncer at a nightclub, trying to protect someone who's already been kicked out of the country. Flores-Ruiz isn't just some harmless individual; he's a guy with multiple counts of domestic abuse-related battery against him. This isn't a minor infraction; this is a dude who poses a danger to the community.

And let's consider the implications of this behavior. When judges start thinking they can pick and choose which laws to enforce based on their personal beliefs, we're opening Pandora's box. What's next? Judges deciding which criminals deserve protection and which don't? That's a slippery slope into chaos. We can't have a judicial system where personal bias trumps the law. If Dugan can help Flores-Ruiz evade arrest, what's stopping other judges from doing the same for other criminals?

This is a fundamental breakdown of what it means to be a judge. When you take that oath, you're supposed to be impartial, to ensure that the law is applied fairly. Instead, Dugan acted like she was above it all, like she could play God with the law.

Now, shifting gears to New Mexico, we have the Cano couple: Judge Jose Cano and his wife, Nancy. They're facing serious charges, too, and let me tell you, they won't result in just a little slap on the wrist. They're knee-deep in some serious trouble, facing up to fifteen years in prison, for allegedly tampering with evidence related to a case involving a Venezuelan national, Cristhian Ortega-Lopez, who has ties to a foreign terrorist organization, the Tren de Aragua gang. That's right, this guy is not just some random immigrant; he's tied to a transnational criminal organization—and the Canos couple thought it was a good idea to help him out. Once again, we're not just dealing with some petty crimes here; we're talking about supporting a suspected gang member who's already shown he's a danger to society.

The charges against the judge and his wife stem from their alleged attempts to hide Ortega-Lopez from law enforcement. They were supposedly helping him evade capture while he was illegally possessing firearms. The feds got tipped off about Ortega-Lopez's illegal presence in the country and his penchant for firearms possession—real charming guy, huh? And what did the Canos couple do? They allegedly tampered with evidence to protect him. That's not just a breach of trust; that's a full-on betrayal of the very principles they swore to uphold.

Let's get specific here. Homeland Security Investigations (HSI) started looking into Ortega-Lopez after receiving a tip that he was unlawfully present in the United States and had firearms. What did they find? Photos and videos on social media showing Ortega-Lopez and other illegal aliens handling firearms at a shooting range. Firearms like a Sig Sauer P365 handgun, an AR-15 rifle with a suppressor, and other high-powered weapons. He even had distinctive tattoos that confirmed his identity.

When HSI executed search warrants related to Ortega-Lopez, they arrested him and confiscated multiple firearms.

But here's where it gets interesting: during the investigation, it was revealed that Nancy Cano was allegedly using multiple phones to communicate with Ortega-Lopez, even facilitating conversations that involved deleting incriminating evidence. And guess what else? Jose Cano, the former judge, admitted to destroying Ortega's cellphone by smashing it with a hammer because he thought it contained incriminating photos and videos. You can't make this stuff up! They were actively trying to cover up Ortega-Lopez's criminal activities, thinking they could just sweep it under the rug.

Let's pause for a moment to think about that. Here's a guy who wore a robe, who was supposed to uphold the law, actively participating in a cover-up. This is the kind of behavior that erodes public trust in the judiciary. When judges start acting like criminals themselves, how can we expect the public to respect the law?

Attorney General Pamela Bondi hit the nail on the head when she stated, "No one, least of all a judge, should obstruct law enforcement operations." Judges are supposed to be the gatekeepers of justice, not the ones trying to sabotage it. They're held to a higher standard for a reason. When you wear that robe, you're not just an authority figure; you're supposed to embody integrity and justice. It's beyond egregious for a former judge and his wife to engage in evidence tampering on behalf of a suspected gang member.

Now, let's go back to Milwaukee, and the case of Judge Dugan. The Justice Department filed a federal criminal complaint against her for allegedly interfering with a federal law enforcement operation, which carries serious charges. She's facing the possibility of five years in prison for obstruction and another year for concealing a person to prevent arrest. So, a judge who is supposed to uphold the law could end up behind bars because she thought she could manipulate the rules.

And consider the fallout from Truthese cases. Deputy Attorney General Todd Blanche made it clear: "Sanctuary jurisdictions that shield criminal aliens endanger American communities." This is a crucial point. When judges like Dugan and the Canos allow their biases to cloud their judgment, they're putting the safety of American citizens at risk. Reckless sanctuary policies don't just create a welcome mat for illegal immigrants; they create a sanctuary for criminals. And if we let this slide, we're opening the door for more of this nonsense.

Now, some want to frame this as Trump's administration going after the judiciary, but that's a load of nonsense. This isn't about politics; it's about accountability. When judges step out of line, they need to face the consequences. Just because you wear a robe doesn't mean you're above the law. The people who are supposed to uphold the law should be held to the highest standards, not afforded special treatment because of their position.

So, here's the bottom line: we need to demand accountability from everyone in the system, from the lowest clerk to the highest judge. If judges can't uphold the law, then they don't belong in the courtroom. It's time to clean house and make sure we have judges who respect the law and understand their role in the justice system.

We're living in a time where the lines between right and wrong are getting blurred, and it's up to us to draw those lines clearly. We can't let judges play fast and loose with the law while pretending they're above it all. It's time for America to stand up, take a hard look at who we're putting in positions of power, and make sure they're held to the highest standards.

Also: this is about more than only judges. It's about the integrity of our entire legal system. We can't allow a few bad apples to spoil the bunch. If we let this kind of behavior continue unchecked, we're setting ourselves up for disaster. It's time to take a stand and demand that our judicial system operates with transparency, accountability, and, most importantly, integrity.

Judges should be held to a higher standard, and if they can't handle that responsibility, then maybe they shouldn't be wearing those robes in the first place. We owe it to ourselves, our communities, and future generations to ensure that justice is served. We can't afford to let the system become a playground for those who think they're above the law. Enough is enough!

Let's get back to basics. Judges should be upholding the law, not undermining it. The integrity of our judicial system depends on it, and we owe it to ourselves and to the legacy we leave behind. This is our call to action, and I'm ready to answer it. Are you?

◆ 37 ◆

THE RISE OF THE COMMON SENSE PARTY

POLITICS, LIKE THE MEDIA, HAS become a circus, and instead of lions and tigers, we've got a bunch of clowns throwing pies at each other while the people are left standing there, wondering when the show is going to end. Well, let me tell you something: the show is over. It's time for the Common Sense Party to take center stage.

Okay, before you roll your eyes and say, "Oh great, another party," let me break it down for you. We've had the Democrats, and we've had the Republicans, and what have they done? They've turned this beautiful country into a battleground where common sense goes to die. It's like watching two kids fight over a toy while we adults stand around waiting for them to grow up. But Donald Trump won in 2024 not because he played into the left-right dynamic, but because he tapped into something much deeper—common sense!

Now, I can hear the critics already. "How can you say that? He's a controversial figure!" And to that, I say, "Of course he is! But controversy is part of the game." Donald Trump isn't your typical politician. Hell, he's not even a politician, in the traditional sense. He's a businessman who walked into the political arena like he owned the place, and honestly? He did it without the usual red tape and nonsense. That's what people respect. They see a guy who's willing to throw politics out the window and just do what's best for the country, based on the situation at hand. That's what commonsense leadership looks like.

Let me tell you about my experiences on the road. When I perform my comedy shows across this great nation, it's always fascinating to see the crowd. They come from all over—young, old, Black, White, Latino, you name it. After the show, people approach me, and the conversations we have are just as entertaining as the jokes I tell. They come up and say, "Tyrus, I don't always agree with everything, but man, you just make sense!" It's refreshing to hear that kind of honesty. It's like I'm holding a mirror up to the audience, and they're finally seeing their own reflections—people who are tired of the extremes and just want to talk about real life.

And let's consider this identity politics nonsense for a second. You know the drill—pick the right person for a job because of their skin color or gender or sexual preference. But let me ask you this: when your house is on fire, do you care if the firefighter is a man, woman, gay, straight, purple, or green? No! You just want them to put out the fire! That's what the Common Sense Party is all about—choosing the right people for the job based on their abilities and experience, not because they check off some box on a diversity chart.

I mean, come on! We've got kids graduating college with degrees in social justice while they can't even change a tire. What happened to good old-fashioned skills? Let's get back to basics. Can you do the job? Great! You're hired. Can you negotiate with other countries? Fantastic! Let's talk trade. When it comes to foreign policy, we need people representing the American people, not their own agenda or some lofty ideal. We need negotiators who are going to stand up for us and say, "Listen, here are the facts. What's best for America is what's best for all of us."

And it's not about being right or left anymore. It's about being smart. The Common Sense Party isn't about taking sides; it's about taking action. If something works, let's use it. If it doesn't, then let's toss it out like last week's leftovers. There's no room for stubbornness; it's time for practicality to take the wheel.

And guess what? Common sense isn't just for the White, middle-aged guy in a suit. It's for everyone! We all have a stake in this game called life. We all want a better future for our kids, for our communities, and for ourselves. So, let's put the right people in charge who want to build bridges, not walls. Let's find leaders who prioritize what's best for the American people over any partisan agenda. This isn't some utopian dream; it's simply common sense.

And you know what? That's why viewers keep tuning in to watch us on TV. It's not because I'm some political savant; it's because I'm the guy who tells it like it is. I give people a voice and validate their commonsense views of the world. After a show in a small town in Middle America, a retired factory worker came up to me, shaking his head and chuckling. He said, "Tyrus, I don't know how you do it. You take all this nonsense, make it funny, and somehow, I feel like I'm not alone in thinking it's all ridiculous." That's the power of the Common Sense Party. It's about connecting with people, and I'm just the messenger, speaking the truth that so many of us already know.

Now, I know some of you are thinking, "Yeah, this sounds great, but how do we make it happen?" Great question. It starts with us. We need to demand better from our leaders. We need to hold them accountable and let them know that we're tired of the same old song and dance. It's time to shake things up and call for a new way of thinking. The Common Sense Party is about uniting people from all walks of life who are fed up with the nonsense and want real solutions.

Look, we live in a time where it's easy to get bogged down in the noise. Social media is a war zone of misinformation and fake news, and it's enough to make your head spin. But that's why we need to come together under a banner of common sense. Let's tune out the chaos and tune into what really matters. It's not about what color your political jersey is; it's about what's good for the country.

So, let's rally the troops. Let's start having conversations that matter. Let's be the generation that stands up and says, "Enough is enough!" We want leaders who are pragmatic, who are going to make decisions that benefit the American people, first and foremost. No more pandering, no more posturing—just good old-fashioned common sense.

It's time for a new movement. The Common Sense Party isn't just a catchy phrase; it's a call to action. Let's rise up and say we want more than just the usual political games. Let's demand leaders who embody the very essence of common sense. It's time to put America back on track, and it starts with us.

◆ 38 ◆

THE DARK WOKE AWAKENING

REMEMBER WHEN THE DEMOCRATIC PARTY was riding high in the summer of 2024? Kamala Harris had just strutted onto the scene as the party's nominee, and for the Democrats everything seemed like a meme-filled dream. Tim Walz was rocking that outdoorsy aesthetic, and the vibe was electric. It was all good...until it wasn't. Fast-forward to today, and it looks like the left is scrambling to find its groove, while Donald Trump is back in the White House, turning the political landscape into a testosterone-fueled showdown.

Here's the thing: the Democrats are trying to shake off the dust of their "earnest resistance" era. You know, that period where they thought the best way to combat Trump's bombastic antics was with polite, high-road platitudes? Yeah, that's so last season. Now, they're looking to embrace a new form of rhetoric—something they're calling "dark woke." This isn't just a catchy phrase; it's an entire strategy that aims to get them back in the game by being just as crass and combative as their opponents.

Let's dissect this "dark woke" nonsense. It's like they took a page out of the "dirtbag left" playbook—those young progressives who don't shy away from throwing shade at anyone in their way, including their own. They're tired of playing nice, and frankly, I can't blame them. But here's where it gets rich: they're now trying to market this as a cool new vibe, like it's some edgy underground band that just dropped a hot album. Sorry to break the news: it's not. It's just a sad attempt to mimic what they think is working for the right.

Let's talk about the term "dark woke" itself. What is that even supposed to mean? It sounds like some kind of bad horror movie—"Darth Woke: The Rise of the Political Correctness." You can practically hear the ominous music playing in the background. And it's offensive. It's like they're saying that something dark is inherently bad or dangerous. As a person of color, I find that deeply problematic. Why do we have to associate something "dark" with negativity? Why not "purple woke"? Or how about "rainbow woke"? Let's get creative, people! This is just another example of how out of touch they are with reality.

And while we're on the subject of being out of touch, let's address the recent voter revolt in San Francisco against the "doom loop" of wokeness. Yes, you heard that right! Even the City by the Bay is rethinking its overly woke policies. They passed four significant ballot proposals that restore some common sense to policing, welfare benefits, and education. How did we get here? A city that once proudly waved the flag of progressive excess is saying, "Hold up, maybe we've gone too far."

One of the measures sets a minimum size for police staffing, allowing cops to chase suspects even when they can't cite an immediate threat to public safety. Let me repeat that: San Francisco is letting cops do their jobs! You'd think they were handing out gold stars for basic law enforcement. They even approved public-safety cameras that use facial recognition tech. I mean, who would've thought that city would embrace technology to actually keep people safe?

Mayor London Breed, once a staunch defunder of the police, is now backing measures that empower law enforcement. She had a lightbulb moment where she realized that "harm reduction" doesn't mean reducing harm; it means doing the hard work to keep people safe. It's a radical idea, I know! It's like she suddenly got the memo that common sense isn't just for conservatives.

But let's not give them too much credit. Just because one person decided to step back from the edge doesn't mean the entire party has changed. The Democrats are still loaded with activists who cling to their ridiculous ideologies. Until they purge that nonsense from their ranks, we're going to keep seeing this "dark woke" rubbish pop up everywhere.

And let's look at the underlying assumption here. The Democrats often choose their "champions" based on stereotypes that they think represent the average American. Who do they pick? George Floyd, MS-13 members, and others whose backgrounds paint a picture of chaos and dysfunction. They believe this is what speaks to the American people because, in their minds, it's what represents the "struggle." They think that by picking these figures, they'll rally the masses behind them. But what they're really doing is insulting the intelligence of the very people they claim to represent.

So, here's the deal: if they keep picking these kinds of so-called champions, they're going to keep losing. The American public isn't dumb. We see right through the manipulation. And when you try to shove a narrative down our throats that includes these questionable figures, well, that's when you lose credibility.

You can't just throw around terms like "dark woke" and expect people to rally around you. You've got to show up with real solutions, not just clever sound bites and memes. The world doesn't need another hashtag-resistance movement that relies on viral clips and snappy comebacks. We need substance, not just style.

As we sit here watching the Democrats flounder and struggle to redefine themselves, let's remember one fundamental truth: it's not about being "dark woke" or any other trendy term they want to slap on their messaging. It's about respect for the American people and understanding what they really want.

And let's not ignore the fact that while they're trying to figure out their new identity, we've got a country in crisis. We've got rising crime rates, homelessness, and a general sense of disarray. The American people want leaders who will tackle these issues, not just engage in petty squabbles and meme wars.

So, to the Democrats still clinging to their "dark woke" dreams, I say this: enough with the theatrics. It's time to roll up your sleeves and do the hard work. Stop pandering to the extremes within your party and start listening to the average American who just wants to feel safe in their community.

We need commonsense solutions that aren't wrapped in political correctness or trendy phrases. The people of San Francisco have shown us that even in the most liberal strongholds, there's a limit to how far you can push "wokeness." It's time for all of us to wake up and demand better—not just from the Democrats, but from everyone in power.

Let's put the "dark woke" nonsense to bed and get back to basics. It's time for accountability, common sense, and a commitment to serving the American people. Because that's what this is all about.

◆ 39 ◆

THE TRUTH BEHIND THE CURTAIN

LET'S NOT COVER IT UP: the term "fake news" has become a cultural punchline. When Donald Trump first threw that grenade into the media landscape, the impact was seismic. It was like a new cuss word, a battle cry against the establishment media that had been lying to the American people for years. But as with any term that gets overused, the meaning has become diluted. Fake news was once a serious accusation, but it's now tossed around so casually that it's lost its sting. It's like the boy who cried wolf—eventually, nobody believes it anymore.

Now, let's draw a more serious historical parallel. When you throw around the name "Hitler," it used to evoke a visceral reaction. That term carried the weight of a monstrous evil. But today? It's dumped into political debates like garbage into a landfill. The value of that term, like "fake news," has eroded. When you call something "fake news," it's more likely to elicit a chuckle than a serious examination of the facts. We've allowed these labels to lose their potency, and that's dangerous.

So, what do we say instead? We need to start calling it what it really is—propaganda. When you say "propaganda," it brings to mind images of manipulation, deceit, and an agenda hidden behind a smiling face. We're not just dealing with the media anymore; we're grappling with a calculated effort by the extreme left to redefine our reality. This isn't merely a matter of miscommunication; it's an all-out assault on the American way of life.

What transpired during the Biden presidency? In my eyes, it was nothing short of a coup—a hostile takeover of the American people and everything we hold dear. A small group of individuals with radical, extreme views infiltrated our government, pushing laws that have far-reaching impacts for generations. They didn't just knock on our door; they kicked it down and started dictating how we should raise our kids and what moral values we should hold dear. They hijacked our freedoms under the guise of safety and unity, and when we finally raised our voices in protest, they shut the country down. They didn't just disrupt our lives; they obliterated an entire generation's education and mental health, tethering them to screens and social media, making them unable to navigate the real world.

These weren't just missteps or mistakes. No, they had a plan, and anyone who dared to speak against it was labeled an enemy of the state. Let's take, for example, the treatment of those who questioned Biden's fitness for office. You couldn't even ask a legitimate question without being branded a conspiracy theorist. The essence of journalism—asking questions and seeking the truth—was thrown out the window in favor of narratives that suited a specific agenda.

The media? They sold out. They chose sides—sides that lined their pockets and bolstered their careers. They turned their backs on the American people and opted for self-interest. And that's a betrayal of the trust that's supposed to exist between a free press and the public. When I say that the media is the head of the snake, I mean it. They thrive on chaos, division, and misinformation. They benefit from the very unrest they propagate. Why? Because it's lucrative. They gain access to power, insider information, and all the perks that come with it—a cushy book deal, a high-profile speaking engagement, or a coveted award. It's a pay-for-play scheme, and we, the American people, are the ones getting played.

So what should we be doing instead? We need to examine every taxpayer dollar that's been misappropriated, scrutinize every executive order that's been signed without proper oversight, and hold these people accountable. The White House has been carjacked, people. We have to go back and reevaluate everything we once thought was merely wild conspiracy theory. Was the election rigged? Were these extreme leftist agendas really as innocuous as they claimed? With the media's track record of deceit, how can we trust anything they say?

We're at a crossroads. We're starting to see the cracks in the façade, and I predict we're going to witness a wave of so-called journalists trying to jump ship. They'll come out with their confessions, scrambling to distance themselves from the very lies they perpetuated. You bet I'm going to write about what I've seen and heard, because someone has to shed light on the truth. The reality is, these people knew what they were doing, and they need to be held accountable.

As I sit in my chair, or I'm driving my truck, I can't help but wonder: how can people not see the blatant greed and corruption right in front of them? It's all about money and power. Look at the misplaced funds over the last few years. Senators who once railed against student loans suddenly find themselves with fat bank accounts. It's a game to them. They were all in on it, playing both sides, and now they're scared because the American people are starting to wise up.

You know the old Ben Franklin saying, "Three people can keep a secret only if two of them are dead"? Well, that's what we're witnessing now. The rats are starting to turn on each other. When the truth begins to emerge, and it will, you'll see the backstabbing commence. Retirements will be announced—not because they want to spend more time with their families, but because they're trying to escape the consequences of their actions.

And there's the media. They wield the power to destroy lives within a single news cycle. One wrong move, one challenge to the narrative, and you're labeled a pariah. If you were a doctor questioning Dr. Fauci, your career was put in jeopardy. The media don't care about fair reporting; they care about controlling the narrative and sustaining their power. They've built a fortress around themselves where dissenting voices are silenced, and that's not how a free society is supposed to function.

Now, did Donald Trump's presence drive this behavior, or was it already in the works? I'd argue his presence accelerated it. The Democrats were so obsessed with taking him down that they lost sight of themselves. They revealed their true nature, which has always been about self-interest at the expense of the American people. It's a business for them, and they don't care who gets hurt along the way.

Trump wasn't just a political opponent; he was a disruptor. He shattered the status quo, and that scared the hell out of the establishment. In their battle against him, the Democrats revealed themselves for what they truly are: a party that prioritizes power over people, profits over principles. They've become so consumed by their obsession with taking him down that they've lost their moral compass. It's a tragic spectacle, but it's also a revealing one.

We're left with a choice: either we reclaim our narrative, or we allow these propagandists to continue their unchecked reign. Who are these "journalists," anyway? We need to start checking IDs at the table of democracy. The extreme left has infiltrated our institutions, and we must stand guard to protect our values and our country.

This isn't just a battle for political control; it's a fight for the soul of America. And I refuse to back down. We have to rise up, challenge the status quo, and hold these people accountable for their actions. The truth may be uncomfortable, but seeking it is the only path forward. We owe it to ourselves, to our children, and to future generations to take a stand against this tide of deceit and corruption.

So let's gear up. It's time to push back, to challenge the narratives, and to reclaim our truth. The next generation deserves to inherit a country that values honesty and integrity, not one mired in lies and corruption. It's time for the American people to rise up and say, "Enough is enough! We're done with the lies, done with the manipulation."

It's time to take back our country, our values, and our future. This is our moment, and we need to seize it.

◆ 40 ◆

CANCEL CULTURE:

THE NEVER-ENDING GAME OF WHACK-A-MOLE

LET'S TALK CANCEL CULTURE, SHALL we? Ah, yes, the phenomenon that's as American as apple pie—if apple pie were served with a side of social-media outrage and a sprinkle of virtue-signaling. After Donald Trump snagged a second term, many folks popped the champagne corks and declared, "Hallelujah! The age of cancel culture is over!" But let me tell you something: that's about as likely as a snowstorm in July. Sure, it might seem like the liberals are taking a breather, like a boxer between rounds, but don't you dare get comfortable. They're just re-strategizing and plotting their next move.

You see, cancel culture isn't just a trend; it's become part of the liberal playbook, like a secret sauce that adds flavor to their narrative. You can't just toss that out because a few people on Twitter (okay, "X") decided to hit the brakes. It's the lifeblood of their party—a way to silence dissent, intimidate the opposition, and create a monolithic information culture where only the approved opinions get airtime. They might wave a white flag, but it's really just a false flag—like when a magician distracts you with one hand while the other hand is busy pulling a rabbit out of a hat.

Now, I'm not one to shy away from a good debate, especially when I'm out on the road, meeting fans after my shows. Whether it's a packed theater in Manhattan or a cozy bar in small-town America, the topic of cancel culture always comes up. It's like asking about the weather; you can't escape it, and everyone has an opinion. I hear stories from folks who've been scared to voice their thoughts at work, people who've had their careers derailed because they dared to express a differing viewpoint. It's a real thing, and it's an epidemic that's spreading faster than a rumor at a family reunion.

But liberals will try to convince you that they're the champions of free speech, while simultaneously throwing a hissy fit if you dare to challenge their narrative. They'll scream about inclusivity while excluding anyone who doesn't toe the party line. Trying to navigate that ever-changing party line is exhausting.

Cancel culture is rooted in intimidation. It's not just about silencing outspoken voices; it's about creating an environment where people are scared to speak up in the first place. You know what I'm talking about—the "you better watch what you say" vibe that hangs in the air like a thick fog. It's a game of psychological warfare, and the left has mastered it like seasoned chess players. They'll play the long game, waiting for the perfect moment to strike, and when they do, it's not pretty.

Imagine you're at a family gathering, and your uncle starts talking about politics. He's got a few hot takes, and you can feel the tension rising as your aunt rolls her eyes, ready to pounce. That's cancel culture in a nutshell. One wrong word, one offhand comment, and suddenly you're the black sheep of the family, the one who needs to be exiled to the corner with the fruitcake. It's a form of social ostracism that's as effective as it is ridiculous.

And let's remember the role social media plays in all of this. Twitter (yeah, yeah—X) might as well be the cancel culture capital of the world. It's where people go to start a mob, armed with hashtags and righteous indignation. You can tweet something innocuous—"I like pineapples on pizza"—and suddenly you're being dragged through the digital mud by a pack of angry keyboard warriors. It's like a virtual witch hunt. And it's not going away anytime soon.

Now, don't get me wrong; I'm all for holding people accountable for their words and actions. But cancel culture takes it to a whole new level. It's not about accountability; it's about annihilation. They don't just want to critique your opinion; they want to erase your existence. They'll go after your job, your reputation, your livelihood—all because they disagree with you. It's a mob mentality, and it's as toxic as it gets.

So, do we just sit back and take it? Hell no! We've got to fight back. We've got to push back against this ridiculous notion that we can't express our opinions without fear of retribution. We need to create a culture where diverse viewpoints are celebrated, not silenced. And that starts with each and every one of us standing up and saying, "Enough is enough!"

But you can't let your guard down. Just because it seems for a minute like the liberals have backed off doesn't mean they're gone. They're regrouping, reloading, and waiting for the right moment to strike. It's like that horror movie where you think the monster is dead, but then it pops back up for one last scare. It's not over until after the credits roll.

When I'm out on the road, I see the fear in people's eyes. They want to share their thoughts, but they're terrified of the consequences. They don't want to be "that guy" who gets called out on social media or loses their job because they dared to express an unpopular opinion. It's a sad state of affairs when people feel like they have to tiptoe around their own beliefs.

But we can't let fear dictate our lives. We're not in a dystopian novel where Big Brother is watching our every move. We're in America, where free speech is supposed to be a fundamental right. So let's reclaim that right. Let's start conversations, challenge each other's ideas, and bring back the art of debate. It's okay to disagree; in fact, it's healthy! It's how we grow and learn.

And to my liberal friends—yes, I'm talking to you—let's have some real talk. We need to stop playing this game of cancel culture. It's not doing anyone any favors. Instead of trying to silence opposing viewpoints, let's engage with them. Let's have tough conversations that make us uncomfortable. It's only through these conversations that we can truly understand each other and find common ground. But if you're more interested in silencing dissent than fostering dialogue, then you're part of the problem.

Finally, we need to realize that cancel culture is a symptom of a larger issue—a growing intolerance for differing opinions. It's a slippery slope that leads to a society where only one narrative is allowed to thrive, and that's a dangerous place to be. So let's keep the conversation going. Let's embrace the messy, chaotic, and sometimes uncomfortable nature of free speech. Because if we don't, we risk losing something far more valuable than a few opinions: we risk losing our very identity as a nation built on the principles of freedom and expression.

So, here's my challenge to all of you: don't just sit there and let cancel culture creep back in. Stand up, speak out, and don't let anyone intimidate you into silence. Whether you're in a small-town diner or a bustling city café, share your thoughts and engage in discussions. Make your voice heard, and let's show the world that we won't be silenced. Because cancel culture may try to take us down, but we're not going anywhere. We'll keep fighting the good fight, one laugh at a time.

Yes, the war against cancel culture is far from over. It's a never-ending game of whack-a-mole, and we're just getting started. So, grab your mallet and let's get to work.

◆ 41 ◆

THE NIGHT I BECAME A PATRIOT (OF SORTS)

SO THERE I WAS, STANDING in front of a room full of heroes—real-life, badge-wearing, cap-crushing, law-enforcing heroes. And me? Just a guy who talks a lot of smack and cracks jokes. And yet, somehow, I found myself being handed the 2024 Patriot of the Year award by the Federal Law Enforcement Officers Foundation. Yeah, that's right. Me. Tyrus. The guy who thinks being "humble" means not wearing my favorite T-shirt to the grocery store.

Honestly, when they first told me I was receiving this award, I was like, "You sure you got the right guy?" I mean, I'm not exactly the poster child for law enforcement. I'm not patrolling the streets; I'm just out here trying to make sense of the chaos and throw some laughter into the mix. But then I walked into that room and saw all those incredible men and women in law enforcement—federal agents, police chiefs, FBI agents, Secret Service, and even the police chief from Israel. I felt like a kid in a candy store, only this candy had badges and guns.

As I stood there, listening to stories of true heroism, I couldn't help but feel a little out of place. There were people who had risked their lives, faced down danger, and done things that would make most of us curl up in a ball and hide under our beds. And here I was, a guy who talks about the absurdity of life on a stage, making people laugh. But then it hit me—maybe that's why I was there. Maybe humor and truth are just as important in this world as a badge and a gun.

When they handed me that beautiful plaque, I felt a mix of pride and confusion. I mean, I was honored, don't get me wrong, but I couldn't help but glance around at the other awards being handed out. I saw these gorgeous Henry rifles—real showstoppers. And I thought to myself, "Man, I want one of those!" I mean, what's cooler than a rifle with your name on it?

So, I made a joke about it during my speech, asking who gets the "cool-ass guns." The room erupted in laughter, and for a second, I thought, "Maybe humor really is the key to bridging the gap." But then they surprised me with my own Henry Big Daddy! Apparently, it was for "obvious reasons." I took that as a compliment, though I'm still not entirely sure what those reasons are!

But it's not just about the awards and the accolades. What I truly cherish about that night was the overwhelming feeling of gratitude and responsibility. I mean, let's be real here. We need to make supporting law enforcement cool again. We need to remind people that those with badges are our heroes—not the fictional ones flying around in capes, but the real ones who stand up for us every day. I said it then, and I'll say it again: we need to make it sexy to be a cop again! We need to know our police officers and engage with our communities.

In a world where everyone wants to be the next rapper or NBA star, let's not forget who you call when things go south.

It's not your favorite artist; it's the police. So, let's start lifting up our law enforcement officers, showing kids that being a firefighter, police officer, or teacher is just as cool—if not cooler—than any unrealistic fantasy the media throw at them.

Aas I was shaking hands and taking pictures with young color guard members who were ready to protect our communities, I felt a surge of hope. These kids were excited, engaged, and not glued to their phones. That's the future I want to see—a future where kids aspire to be heroes in their own right, not just players in a game or characters in a movie.

But back to the award. I mean, why me? I'm just a guy who shares what's on my mind. I'm not a philosopher or a poet, and yet somehow, the things I say resonate with people. That's humbling. Really humbling. It's like, "Hey man, I just exercised my freedom of speech, and you're rewarding me for it?" That's a strange kind of gratitude to carry around.

And this wasn't my first rodeo with awards. I got another Patriot Award at Mar-a-Lago, standing next to legends like Mike Tyson and Mel Gibson. It's wild! I mean, one minute you're cracking jokes on a podcast, and the next you're being recognized by people who put their lives on the line every day.

But what made this night even more significant was the impact it has had on my kids. They got to see firsthand that law enforcement respects me, and, let's be honest, coming from a tough upbringing where I've been on the wrong side of the law a few times, that means a lot. It's a powerful message for them to witness—seeing someone who speaks his mind, who's upfront and truthful, getting acknowledged by those who wear the badge.

Moments like this make me pinch myself and wonder if it's all real. I mean, I've had my share of interesting experiences in life, and I genuinely appreciate the kindness of strangers, but this one hit differently. It was a reminder that, even with my background, I can still earn respect and recognition by simply being me.

So, as I left that night, plaque in hand and a new rifle, to boot, I felt a wave of humility wash over me. I may not wear a badge, but I sure as hell respect those who do, and I'm grateful for the chance to support them in any way I can. This award isn't just mine; it belongs to everyone who stands up for what's right.

Let's make sure we do that together, because—who knows? Maybe one day, we'll all be heroes in our own stories... no capes required.

• 42 •

FROM THE ROAD TO REALITY:

THE DEMOCRATS AND THEIR FAR-LEFT FRINGE

LET ME START BY SAYING this: I've been on the road so much with my one-man show that I feel like P.T. Barnum, minus the elephants and with a lot more opinions. I've hit states from Michigan to Florida, Nebraska to the far reaches of Southern and Northern California and the Pacific Northwest, and let me tell you: the conversations I've had with everyday Americans are eye-opening. You think you know what people are feeling? You don't. Not until you're out there, knee-deep in the real world, talking to folks who are living their lives, not just tweeting about them.

And everyone is saying the same thing. It doesn't matter if they're wearing a "Make America Great Again" hat or a "Feel the Bern" T-shirt. People are fed up with the Democrats.

Now, let me clarify. I'm not here to demonize the entire party. There are still old-school Democrats out there who remember how to have a conversation. They remember what it's like to respect the other side. But the party? Oh boy, they've sold their collective souls to the far-left fringe, and it's starting to show.

I hear it everywhere. In a diner in Michigan, a waitress poured my coffee and said, "You know, I used to vote Democrat, but they've lost touch." In Nebraska, a farmer leaned against his tractor and said, "I don't know what they're smoking, but it's not what we need." Even in the land of palm trees and Hollywood dreams, I get people shaking their heads, saying, "The party doesn't represent me anymore." And here's the truth: they're right.

The Democrats can point fingers at the media all they want, but it's not the media causing their problems. It's their own inability to recognize that they've become prisoners of their fringe. The far left has taken the wheel, and instead of steering toward common ground, they've driven the party right off a cliff. They've embraced cancel culture, where every word is scrutinized, and if you dare to think differently, you might as well be wearing a target on your back.

What happened to the days when you could have a conversation without someone pulling out their digital pitchfork? The far-left fringe can be really loud. They're like that one friend who shows up to a barbecue and insists on talking about veganism while everyone else is just trying to enjoy their burgers. But everyday Americans are tired of the noise. They don't want to be part of a culture that punishes them for simply having an opinion. And that's where the Democrats have gone wrong.

Now, I'm not saying the right side of the aisle has it all figured out. They've got their own issues, believe me. But one thing you can say about them is that they don't cower in fear of groupthink. Donald Trump made it clear: we will not kowtow to the fringe. We will not be pressured into silence. And guess what? That resonates with people. It also resonates with those old-school Democrats who feel like strangers in their own party.

You want to talk about why more and more Democrats are crossing the aisle? It's simple. They're sick of being scared. They're tired of watching their lives get turned upside down for simply thinking differently. They see the right as a space where they can voice their thoughts without fear of being canceled or ridiculed. They're looking for a place where they can engage in a real conversation, not just a shouting match filled with hashtags and outrage.

I've met plenty of people who used to identify as Democrats but now feel alienated by the party's radical shift. They tell me stories about how their friends have unfriended them on social media for daring to express a different opinion. They miss the days when you could disagree without it becoming a personal vendetta. They miss the days when the party stood for something that felt more grounded in reality.

Let's be blunt: the far-left fringe is a loud bunch, and they've managed to create an atmosphere of fear. Fear of saying the wrong thing. Fear of expressing a different opinion. Fear of being labeled. And what does that lead to? A culture of silence. It leads to people nodding along to things they don't actually believe just to avoid the wrath of the mob. And that's not democracy; that's a dictatorship of the loudest voices.

The Democrats need to wake up and smell the coffee—or maybe they should take a cue from the baristas who serve it. People want authenticity. They want leaders who can have real conversations, not just chant political talking points. They want to feel heard, not just be pandered to. But now, the far-left fringe is drowning out the voices of everyday Americans who are just trying to navigate life.

I've seen this firsthand. After a show, I often hang out and chat with people. Some of these people are lifelong Democrats, and they're frustrated. They come up to me with concerns, with stories of how they feel marginalized by their own party. They don't want to see their party lose sight of the values that made them proud to be Democrats in the first place. They want to see a return to fundamentals: respect, dialogue, and a commitment to serving all Americans.

But instead, they're left with a party that seems more concerned with appeasing the loudest voices than actually listening to the average voter. The Democrats have become so enamored with the fringe that they've forgotten about the base. And that's a recipe for disaster.

The longer they ignore this reality, the more they'll continue to alienate the very people they claim to represent. And if you're a politician who can't connect with the ones who put you in office, what are you even doing? It's like a chef who can't cook for their customers. They stop showing up to eat what you're serving. You've got to know your audience, and right now, the Democrats are missing the mark.

So, what's the solution? It's simple: they need to stand up to the far-left fringe and remind them that their radical ideas don't represent the majority. They need to reclaim their party from the loudest voices and return to the values that actually matter to everyday Americans. They need to start having real conversations, not just performative ones where they pat themselves on the back for being "woke."

But at the moment, they're too scared. They're too scared to stand up to the mob they've helped create. They're too scared to risk losing their positions in a party that's become more about ideology than reality. And that fear is paralyzing. It's a fear that's keeping them from reconnecting with the very voters they need to thrive as a party.

And that's why I think we're going to see more and more Democrats crossing the aisle. They're looking for a place where they can speak their minds without fear. They're looking for a place where they can feel like part of a community, not just a cog in a political machine. And the right is more than happy to welcome them with open arms.

This isn't just about politics; it's about people. It's about the everyday American who wants to feel heard and valued. It's about the conversations we have around the dinner table and the respect we show one another, even when we disagree. It's about finding common ground in a world that seems increasingly divided.

So, Democrats, if you really want to repair your party, listen up. It's time to take a long, hard look in the mirror and ask yourselves who you're really serving. It's time to stop pandering to the fringe and start engaging with the base that put you in power in the first place. Otherwise, you might just find yourselves on the wrong side of history—lost in a sea of angry tweets and canceled dinners.

That is the cold hard truth. If you want to be a party that represents all Americans, you've got to start acting like it. Otherwise, you might as well pack up and call it a day. Because everyday Americans are ready for change, and they're not going to wait around for you to figure it out. They're ready for a party that actually listens, respects, and, dare I say, understands them.

Here's hoping the Democrats can get their act together. And if they don't? Well, let's just say the road ahead is going to be a lot bumpier than they think. And I'll be right here, coffee in hand, ready to call out the nonsense when I see it. Because that's what we do. We talk. We laugh. We disagree. And above all else, we stay real.

◆ 43 ◆

HARD TIMES AND THE ROAD AHEAD

WELL, HERE WE ARE. THE world feels like it's been turned upside down, but this is just the beginning. We're in the thick of it right now, and if you think we've seen it all, just wait. We're unearthing decades—no, generations—of corruption, and it's not pretty. You've got new millionaires popping up, senators and congressmen who've made their fortunes funneling and laundering tax dollars, and it's only going to get uglier from here. When the arrests start happening, that's when you'll really see the storm brewing.

The importance of patience in this process can't be overstated. We've allowed ourselves to be dumbed down by mainstream media and a corrupted government. It's become clear that the system is rigged, and the people we've elected have been profiting off our ignorance. I like to call this the "hard times" we're going through. You know, my old wrestling mentor, the iconic Dusty Rhodes, used to talk about hard times, about the struggles you have to endure to achieve something meaningful. If you want to be a champion, you've got to start from the bottom and face adversity. That's the only way you can truly appreciate what you achieve.

Now, let's talk about President Trump. The man has had his fair share of hard times. He's been through the wringer, trying to keep himself, his family, and his business afloat against a tidal wave of corruption. The entire weight of the corrupt government has been pressing down on him, and you have to ask yourself: when did all this start? There was a time when Trump was one of the most beloved figures in the Democratic Party. They were all over him—he was their go-to guy, their donor, their friend. He was like their Beyoncé, always invited to the party. And then, suddenly, everything changed.

Why? Because he decided he wanted out. He saw the corruption and wanted to change things for the better. That's where the bitterness comes in. The Democratic Party didn't like that he wanted to walk away from their shady dealings. It's like when I had a buddy, and we were involved in something illegal together. I realized it wasn't for me, and I wanted out. That's when the resentment started. My friends looked at me like I was the problem, because I knew too much. I was the one who could expose their dirty secrets.

And that's what we're seeing with Trump. It's not merely "Trump Derangement Syndrome"; it's a primal fear from the establishment that someone who knows their dirty laundry might spill it. They had to make him into a monster because he was no longer playing their game. They had to convince everyone that he was the bad guy because they couldn't afford for him to succeed.

This is all about survival for them. It's the same old story. When you're at the top and someone threatens your position, you do whatever it takes to take them down. So, they demonized him. They focused on his personality, his language, his choices. They twisted everything he did into a scandal. They made the world believe that he was a toxic figure, a danger to society. This was their strategy—distract the public from the real issues.

And boy, did they succeed. They turned the American spirit into a battleground. Masculinity became a dirty word. Wanting to be a traditional family man who loves his wife and raises kids? Suddenly, that's a problem. It's a crazy world we're living in when you can't even be proud of who you are without being labeled as the enemy.

These hard times are also about the suppression of traditional values. If you were a man who believed in hard work, respect, and family, you were suddenly in the crosshairs. The so-called "progressives" have created a world where if you don't fit their mold, you're ostracized. They've lumped everyone together—men, women, LGBTQ+—as if we all share the same problems and perspectives. But the reality is far more complex.

And it's not just about identity politics. They've weaponized everything. If I stand up and say something that goes against the grain, I'm a racist, a misogynist, or a homophobe. They've created a culture of fear where speaking your mind comes with real consequences. You could lose your job, your friends, your reputation—all for simply stating your opinion.

What's worse is that the media have been complicit in this. To distract us from the real problems, they've focused on the minutiae—like Trump's taxes, or his property values, or his mean tweets—while ignoring the real issues affecting the American people. Inflation skyrocketed, our electric bills went through the roof, and we were all left to fend for ourselves. Meanwhile, our government was cutting checks for ridiculous studies and projects that had nothing to do with the average American's life.

When the pandemic hit, it only got worse. They were throwing money around like horny frat boys in a brothel while the rest of us struggled to put food on the table. We were worried about toilet paper and formula while they were busy pushing their agenda. They were more concerned with their narratives than with the real problems facing our country.

And they had the audacity to force vaccines and restrictions on us while they themselves were living large. It was a blatant violation of our freedoms, all in the name of "public safety."

Remember, when I talk about hard times, I'm not just speaking in abstract terms. I'm talking about the reality that many Americans face daily. The anxiety of wondering how to make ends meet, the frustration of watching our government waste our tax dollars, the anger that boils over when you see your neighbor's struggles mirrored in your own. This isn't just a political battle; it's a personal one.

Those are the hard times I'm talking about.

But here's where it gets interesting. You see, hard times reveal character. They expose who we really are. When you're faced with adversity, you either fold, or you rise up. You either let the system break you, or you fight back. And I can tell you this: there are millions of Americans who have had enough.

The beauty of hard times is that they force us to reevaluate what we truly value. They remind us that we're stronger when we stand together. We're not just a bunch of disparate groups fighting for scraps; we're Americans, and we can rise up against any challenge.

I think it was around seventy-seven million of us in the 2024 election who stood up and said, "No more. We're not going to be silenced. We're tired of being told what to think and how to feel. We're ready to take our country back." And to President Trump's credit, he's understood that sentiment, and he turned it into his mission. It's not about his legacy; it's about solving problems and making those hard times worth it for everyone.

We're at a point now where we can look back and see that we took those hard times and turned them into opportunities for growth. We're not just sitting on the sidelines anymore; we're getting into the game. We're learning about the stock market, getting involved in local politics, and taking charge of our lives.

We're fired up. We're training, physically and mentally. We're shadowboxing against the bullshit that's been thrown our way. We're revitalizing our spirits, and we're ready to reclaim what's rightfully ours. This country is filled with potential, and we are finally recognizing that.

This is our moment to embrace the hard times and use them as fuel. We have the power to reshape this country into what we know it can be—a place where hard work is rewarded, where family values are respected, and where the American dream is alive and well.

As we move into this next phase, let's remember that change takes time. We didn't get here overnight, and we won't solve everything overnight, either. But we can't lose sight of our goals. We have to keep fighting for our freedoms, our values, and our future.

Let's be clear: it's time to be patient, but that doesn't mean we sit idly by. We've been conditioned to believe that if we can just be patient, everything will work itself out. But patience doesn't mean passivity. It doesn't mean sitting on your hands and hoping for change. It means being prepared, being aware, and being willing to act when the moment is right.

Look around you. The world is changing, and not always for the better. But within that chaos lies opportunity. There are people out there who are hungry for change, who are ready to roll up their sleeves and put in the work. And that's what we need—people who are willing to dig deep and fight for what they believe in.

I know it's tough. I see it every day. People are tired, frustrated, and fed up. But this is where we can make the difference. This is where we can rise above the noise and make our voices heard. We have to hold our leaders accountable and demand that they serve the people, not their own interests.

And then there's the younger generation. They're the future of this country, and it's our responsibility to guide them. We need to teach them the value of hard work, the importance of critical thinking, and the necessity of standing firm in their beliefs. If we don't, we risk losing everything we hold dear.

So, as we navigate these hard times, let's remember that we are not alone. We're in this together, and together we can create a movement that's larger than any one individual. We can build a future that honors our past while looking forward to a brighter tomorrow.

Let's capitalize on this momentum and channel it into action. We're fighting for more than just political change; we're fighting for the soul of our nation. And that's a fight worth having.

Now is the time to put our differences aside and unite for a common purpose. It's time to take a stand and demand the kind of leadership that reflects our values. We need to be the change we want to see. So, stand up, speak out, and let's get to work. We have a lot to do, and together, we can turn these hard times into a legacy of strength and resilience. Let's show them what we're made of. The road ahead may be tough, but we're tougher. And that's something they can't take away from us.

Now, let's get to work.

◆ 44 ◆

BOMBING CARTELS AND SHAKING UP DC:
THE REALITIES OF THE DRUG WAR

LET'S GET ONE THING STRAIGHT right off the bat: no one's losing sleep if a cartel gets bombed. Seriously. The only ones who'll be losing sleep are the cartel members themselves, and frankly, they should be. When you're dealing drugs and ruining lives, you don't get a whole lot of sympathy from the average American. So why are we tiptoeing around these criminals? Why are we acting like they're some misunderstood artists who just need a hug and a little understanding? No, they need a wake-up call, and I mean that literally.

I'll never forget the night President Trump was on our show. It was electric. I asked him a question that had been bouncing around in my head: "Hey, would you consider labeling drug dealers from other countries as terrorist organizations?" You know, so we could take some of the pressure off law enforcement and let the military handle these guys like they're supposed to. And guess what? He didn't flinch. He said, "Yeah, let's do it!" Now, that's the kind of response you want to hear from someone in charge.

Look, I'm not saying we need to go all out and start dropping bombs left and right, but let's face it: if you're running a cartel, you're not exactly a pillar of society. These guys are making billions off the backs of addicts and the suffering of countless families. They're the ones who have turned neighborhoods into war zones, and they're the ones profiting while the rest of us pick up the pieces. If we need to blow a few of them up to send a message, then so be it. You think the Taliban learned their lesson when Trump walked in and slapped down that Polaroid of their hideout? You bet your sweet behind they did!

He made it clear: "That's your house, and I'll blow it up if you even think about messing with one American soldier." You think the Taliban were like, "Oh, no problem, we'll just go back to our day jobs"? Nah, they got the message loud and clear. The same principle applies to these cartels. If they know there's a real threat hanging over their heads, they're going to think twice before trying to mess with the USA.

You keep hearing this phrase: "Trump Derangement Syndrome." Well, it's not Trump Derangement Syndrome; it's the sound of criminals and corrupt politicians freaking out because their gravy train is about to get derailed. They're not upset because Trump is some kind of boogeyman; they're upset because he's coming for their wallets.

These cartels have been living the high life, and they've got their hands in the pockets of plenty of folks in DC. Don't think for a second that there aren't people there looking the other way while cash changes hands. It's not just the drug addicts who are the problem; it's the whole system that's been enabling this madness.

Want the truth? The blowback from any action we take against these cartels isn't going to come from Mexico. Oh no, it's going to come from the very politicians right here in Washington who have been getting cozy with them. They've been living large off the proceeds of this drug trade, and now they see their whole way of life about to change. They're the ones who should be worried, not the guys down south.

And you know what? They've gotten so comfortable that they're willing to come up with the most absurd justifications for their cozy relationship with the cartels. You hear things like, "Well, the cartel donates to petting zoos on the weekends." Seriously? That's the best they can come up with? "Oh, they might be drug lords, but they also care about animals!" It's almost comical if it weren't so sad. This is the kind of nonsense that gets thrown around to distract from the real issue: these are criminals who have made a fortune at the expense of American lives.

Let's consider the real victims here. It's not just the families of addicts who suffer; it's everyone who has to deal with the fallout from the drug trade. It's the communities that are ripped apart by violence, the kids who grow up in neighborhoods where they can't even play outside because of the danger lurking around every corner. It's the police officers who are stretched thin trying to manage the chaos while the politicians in DC sit back and rake in the cash.

So, when we start talking about bombing cartels, it's not just about sending a message; it's about protecting American families and communities. It's about taking a stand against the people who have turned our streets into battlegrounds. It's about making it clear that we're not going to let them continue to profit off the pain of our citizens.

Now, I'm not saying we need to go to full-on military-style operations without thinking it through. We need strategy, we need intelligence, and we need to be smart about how we approach this. But let's not kid ourselves into thinking that these cartels are just misunderstood entrepreneurs. They're ruthless criminals who will do anything to maintain their power and wealth. And if we have to start dropping bombs on their heads to send a message, then let's get serious about it.

And let's not forget about the politicians who are now scrambling to cover their tracks. They're the ones who have been cozying up to these cartels, turning a blind eye to their activities while lining their own pockets. As soon as Trump starts making moves to disrupt their cozy little setup, they flip the script and start acting like they're concerned citizens. Give me a break! They've been part of the problem, and they know it.

These politicians are the ones who should be sweating bullets. They're the ones who have gotten rich off the suffering of others, and now they're seeing the writing on the wall. They're scared because they know that their whole way of life is about to change. But they're not going to give up their mansions and their perks without a fight.

So, when you see these politicians trying to dismiss Trump's actions as "crazy" or "dangerous," remember that they're not worried about national security. They're worried about their wallets. They're worried about losing their influence and their power. They're worried about the money that's been flowing into their campaigns from the very criminals they've been enabling.

And that's where we come in. We need to stay vigilant. We need to keep pushing back against the nonsense and the distractions. The answer, as always, is to hold these politicians accountable for their actions and demand that they start putting the American people first. We can't let them continue to profit off our pain while pretending to be the heroes in this story.

In the end, this isn't just about cartels and bombs; it's about justice. It's about standing up for the families who have lost loved ones to addiction and violence. It's about making sure that the criminals who are wreaking havoc on our streets understand that their time is up.

So, if it takes a bomb or two to send that message, then let's make it happen. Let's stop coddling these criminals and start holding them accountable for the destruction they've caused. Because when it comes down to it, if we don't take a stand now, we're just going to let them keep running the show, and that's not the America I want to live in.

It's time to get serious about this fight. It's time to recognize that we're up against some powerful forces, and we can't let them continue to hold sway over our lives. We need to be loud, we need to be clear, and we need to be unafraid to take action. Because if we don't, we're just going to be stuck in a cycle of violence and corruption that benefits no one but the criminals at the top. It's time to take charge, and I don't know about you, but I'm ready to fight. Bombs away!

◆ 45 ◆

SILVER FOXES AND THE WISDOM OF EXPERIENCE

DOING MY ONE-MAN SHOW, I'M always learning. One of the best parts of this gig is meeting people—especially the older generation. I call them my "silver foxes," and they are a treasure trove of stories, wisdom, and a little bit of mischief. It's a beautiful opportunity to connect with folks who have lived through decades of life experiences, and I think we don't appreciate them enough.

When I perform, I see a crowd filled with laughter and joy, but it's the older people who often leave the biggest impression. They come up to me after the show, sharing snippets of their lives, and I'm always blown away by the richness of their stories. These people have lived three or four lifetimes in just one, witnessing the world change in ways I can only imagine. They've seen everything from the moon landing to the rise of the internet, and their memories are like living history books.

Take, for example, the couple who met in a malt shop back in the day. They tell me how they fell in love over milkshakes and jukebox tunes, and now they've been married for fifty years. I think about how they should write instructional books for the rest of us on how to make relationships last. Their stories often include hard times, too—like when they didn't know where their next meal was coming from. But instead of bitterness, they talk about pulling themselves up by their bootstraps, starting businesses, and raising families. Their resilience is inspiring.

As I travel, I also encounter many veterans who have served in wars from World War II to Vietnam. These men and women wear their experiences like badges of honor. I met one gentleman in a diner in a small town in Ohio who had fought in the Korean War. He was in his late eighties, and every wrinkle on his face told a story. He shared how he had been sent overseas at a young age, far from home, and how those years shaped his understanding of duty, sacrifice, and honor. He spoke about the camaraderie among soldiers, the bonds they formed under fire, and how those relationships still mattered to him decades later.

These veterans often hold the same values that seem to define the spirit of America: hard work, resilience, and a deep love for their country. They remind me that the freedoms we enjoy today were fought for by people who truly understood the weight of sacrifice. Their stories are filled with moments of bravery, but also of vulnerability. One Vietnam veteran I met in a theater lobby shared how he struggled with his experiences long after the war was over. He talked about the importance of community, and how he found healing in sharing his story. His honesty was refreshing, and I realized that even the toughest among us have a softer side.

I remember one particular night in Arkansas that perfectly encapsulated this experience. It was a special show, because a ninety-nine-year-old woman—let's call her my "birthday queen"—came out with her family to celebrate her big day. They rolled in like a parade of tall, beautiful Scandinavian women—blonde hair, from grandma to granddaughters. When she approached me after the show, I could hardly believe she was ninety-nine. She looked like she could pass for sixty, no walker needed, just a sparkle in her eye that told me she was still very much alive at heart.

She said she attended my show to relive a moment from her past—a Billy Joel concert back in the '70s. I was intrigued. I mean, who wouldn't want to hear about a ninety-nine-year-old throwing her panties at a rock star? Yeah, you heard me right. She recounted how she was front row at that concert, and in a moment of youthful spontaneity, she tossed her underwear at Billy Joel. I was both flabbergasted and amused, trying to picture this vibrant grandmother in her prime, the life of the party.

Then she dropped a bombshell on me. "You know," she said, "I brought an extra pair tonight." My heart stopped. Was she about to throw her underwear at me? Thankfully, she paused, laughed, and then said, "But I didn't throw them at you because I laughed so hard I peed! So I had to switch underwear!" The crowd erupted in laughter, and I was left with my mouth agape, trying to process the hilarity of it all.

This woman, who had lived through so much, reminded me of the importance of laughter and joy at any age. She spoke about her family's immigrant roots, how they had to be sponsored to come to America, and the pride they took in each generation improving upon the last. Her daughters went to college, and her granddaughters were now pursuing their own dreams. It was a beautiful reminder of the legacy we all create, piece by piece.

The older generation often embodies a spirit of gratitude and resilience that I find refreshing. They understand the value of work and the importance of family and community. I met a couple in their seventies who had been high school sweethearts. They shared how they faced their challenges together, from raising children to navigating financial hardships. Their love story was one of unwavering support, and I couldn't help but think that their bond was what made them so strong.

At another show, I met a World War II veteran who had stormed the beaches of Normandy. He was soft-spoken but had a presence that commanded respect. He shared stories of bravery and sacrifice, but also spoke about the friends he lost along the way. The emotion in his voice was palpable, and I could see the weight of those memories still resting on his shoulders. When he finished, I stood there, humbled and grateful for his service. It reminded me that our freedoms come at a cost, and it's vital to honor those who made sacrifices to protect them.

One of the most striking aspects of meeting these older citizens is their shared sense of humor. It's a reminder that laughter transcends age. I've had several interactions where their wit caught me off guard. Like the time I met a retired schoolteacher who had a sharp tongue and an even sharper sense of humor. She told me how she would keep her students in line by threatening to unleash her "inner lioness" on them. I laughed so hard, I almost cried. Here was this little old lady, but she had a spirit that could light up a room.

And then there was the great-grandfather who had a knack for storytelling. He spun tales of his childhood during the Great Depression, and it was incredible to hear how he and his siblings made their own fun with nothing but a stick and a bit of imagination. "You wouldn't believe the adventures we had," he said, his eyes twinkling. "We could turn a cardboard box into a spaceship, and a rainy day was just another excuse to build a fort." It made me think about how creativity flourishes in tough times and how those memories shape the people we become.

As I travel, I often reflect on how these older people carry with them a lifetime of lessons. They've seen the world evolve, faced challenges we can only read about, and yet they still find joy in the little things—like a good laugh or a night out with family. Their stories are not just about the past; they are a blueprint for the future.

The fortitude of this generation is something I admire deeply. They've weathered storms—both literal and metaphorical—and emerged with a sense of gratitude. I met a woman in her eighties who had lost her husband a few years back. Instead of dwelling on the sadness, she focused on the life they built together and the adventures they had. "Life is too short to be anything but grateful," she said, and I couldn't agree more. In a world that often rushes past, it's the wisdom of our elders that grounds us, teaches us, and connects us all.

So, when I'm up on that stage, sharing my own stories and making people laugh, I'm grateful for the silver foxes in the audience. They remind me that life is rich with experiences, laughter is timeless, and every person has a story worth hearing. In a world that often rushes past, it's the wisdom of our elders that grounds us, teaches us, and connects us all.

As I wrap up my tour, those stories—the laughter, the resilience, the unexpected moments—stay with me. They are the heart of what I do. I may be the one on stage, but it's the audience, especially those silver foxes, who teach me the most about life. And as I hit the road again, I'll continue to carry their stories with me, hoping to share their laughter and wisdom with others. After all, these silver foxes are not just a part of the audience; they are the backbone of our society. They've lived through it all and come out the other side with lessons we all need to hear.

So here's to them, and to the beautiful, messy, and hilarious journey we call life. Here's to the silver foxes, the veterans, the storytellers, and the dreamers—may their voices continue to resonate with us all.

◆ 46 ◆

THE BAD NEWS BEARS AND THE REALITIES OF YOUTH SPORTS

AS I SIT ON THE sidelines, watching my son play youth baseball, I can't help but feel a torrent of nostalgia mixed with a healthy dose of frustration. The sun beats down, kids are yelling, and the smell of popcorn wafts through the air. It's a chaotic scene, one that's both familiar and comforting. But it also reminds me of a film that has shaped how I view youth sports: the 1976 classic, *The Bad News Bears*. In a world where everyone's tiptoeing around feelings and nobody wants to offend anyone, I can't shake the feeling that a film like this wouldn't stand a chance of being made today. And that's a damn shame, because the raw, unfiltered truth it presents is more relevant than ever.

Morris Buttermaker, played by Walter Matthau, is a hard-drinking, foul-mouthed bum. He guzzles beer, smokes cigars like a chimney, and doesn't give a rat's ass about political correctness. He even takes a martini from one of his underage players. But he's not supposed to be a role model; he's a reflection of reality. The guy knows baseball and understands kids better than most parents do today. He's rough around the edges, but that's what makes him relatable. He embodies the kind of adult that kids can see through—someone who's flawed, real, and, most importantly, honest.

Watching my son on that field brings back memories. Kids are perceptive; they can sniff out your bullshit from a mile away. If you're more worried about your own glory or your phone than about their growth, they'll see it. Buttermaker gets that. When Tanner Boyle, his foul-mouthed shortstop, gets hurt during a game, Buttermaker finally shows some concern. "Tanner. You okay?" he asks, but Tanner fires back, "Look, you crud, just get back to your beer." That's the kind of moment that makes you realize kids aren't stupid. They know what you care about, and if it's not them, they're going to call you out on it.

The film isn't just about a ragtag baseball team; it's a commentary on the pressures that come with youth sports. There's a scene where Ahmad, one of Buttermaker's players, strips off his uniform after a humiliating 26–0 loss and climbs a tree in despair. "Don't deserve to wear no uniform," he says. Buttermaker climbs up to talk him down, and instead of coddling him, he gives him a dose of reality. "Thank God Hank Aaron didn't act like this," he says, reminding Ahmad that even legends had rough starts. It's that tough love that resonates. It's not about coddling kids; it's about teaching them to face adversity like an adult would.

This movie encapsulates the spirit of youth sports, portraying the grit, grind, and spirit of teamwork in a way that feels authentic. But I'm telling you, you wouldn't get away with that today. Even if it somebody could manage to produce it, *The Bad News Bears* would get torn apart by the sensitivity police for its language and its unfiltered portrayal of flawed adults. But there's nothing offensive about it. A few strong words? So what? That's part of life. We've created a culture where we're so afraid of offending someone that we've lost the ability to speak honestly.

Take the scene where Buttermaker tries to lift the team's spirits after another brutal loss. "Rome wasn't built in a day," he quips, only to be hit back with, "It took several hundred years." The banter is real, and it's a reminder that failure isn't the end of the world. Kids need to learn that it's okay to stumble, to fall, and to get back up again. That's how you build character.

There's something else that stands out in *The Bad News Bears*: the underdog spirit. Buttermaker's team is a ragtag group of misfits who, frankly, have no business being on a baseball diamond. But they come together, and they learn to support each other. They fight, they fail, and they eventually find a way to enjoy the game. There's a beautiful lesson in that. In this world, you've got to learn to rely on your teammates, and sometimes that means putting your own ego aside.

One of the most memorable moments is when the team votes to quit after a series of humiliating losses. But Buttermaker isn't having it. "This quitting thing, it's a hard habit to break once you start," he tells them. That's the kind of grit we need to instill in our kids. It's not just about the game; it's about life. Quitting is easy, but pushing through is what builds character. The kids don't realize it at first, but they're learning a valuable lesson about perseverance, one that will serve them well beyond the baseball diamond.

And what about Amanda Whurlitzer, the girl pitcher who shows them all how it's done. She's tough, she can throw a curveball better than most of the boys, and no one gives her grief about it. The movie made it clear: talent doesn't have a gender. It's a lesson that's just as important now as it was then.

One of the most glaring realities of youth sports today is the prevalence of over-involvement from parents. We've all seen the dad who's living vicariously through his kid, yelling from the sidelines as if he's in the big leagues himself. Buttermaker represents the anti-parent hero in this scenario. He's not there to fulfill his own dreams; he's there to coach these kids, even if his methods are unconventional. His indifference to the win-at-all-costs mentality is refreshing. "I haven't been much of a manager...or much of anything else, for that matter," he admits. That's the kind of honesty we need more of in youth sports.

There's also a crucial lesson about camaraderie and teamwork woven throughout the film. Buttermaker's team doesn't just learn to play baseball; they learn to trust each other. When Timmy Lupus, arguably the worst player on the team, is put in the outfield during the championship game, everyone's nervous. But Buttermaker tells him, "Listen, Lupus, you didn't come into this life just to sit around on a dugout bench, did you? Get your ass out there and do the best you can." That moment is critical; it's not about being the best player; it's about being part of something bigger.

And when Timmy makes a miraculous catch at the right field fence, robbing the Yankees of a home run, it's more than just a great moment in the game; it's a testament to the idea that everyone has a role to play. This is the essence of teamwork. You never know who's going to step up when it counts, and giving everyone a chance to shine is what makes a team truly special. Buttermaker's unorthodox coaching style allows his players to discover their strengths, and that's a lesson that resonates long after the final out is called.

It's about life skills. *The Bad News Bears* teaches kids to deal with disappointment, to learn from their mistakes, and to celebrate each other's successes. When the Bears finally come together as a team, it's not because they've suddenly become all-stars; it's because they've learned to enjoy playing the game together. That's the kind of spirit we need to instill in our kids today. Youth sports should be a space for growth, resilience, and camaraderie. It should be about finding joy in the game, just like *The Bad News Bears* taught us. It's not about being perfect; it's about being real.

◆ 47 ◆

THE RECKONING OF SILENCE

IT'S TIME ONCE AGAIN TO pull back the curtain on the charade that was the Biden presidency and call out every last person who defended it. So, let's examine the usual suspects: Jen Psaki, Joe Scarborough, Jake Tapper, the cast of *The View*, and the late-night comedians who thought it was clever to make excuses for a man who was, quite frankly, a walking disaster.

The level of dishonesty we witnessed from these so-called public figures is unprecedented. They stood by, nodding along, while Joe Biden stumbled through his presidency like a man lost in a fog. And while they were patting each other on the back, the American people were left to sift through the fallout of their blind allegiance.

Let's kick it off with Jen Psaki. The woman who was supposed to be the voice of transparency, but instead became the queen of deflection. Every time she sidestepped a question with a practiced smile, she was doing a disservice to the American people. We saw you, Jen. We heard you spin the narrative, twisting facts into pretzel shapes to defend the indefensible. When Biden fumbled through speeches and made incoherent statements, you were there, ready with a smile and a talking point, as if that would make everything better. It's pathetic, really.

And then there's Joe Scarborough. The man who used to claim he was a Republican but has morphed into a caricature of himself on MSNBC. Scarborough, with his smug smirk, spent years trying to convince us that Biden was the best option we had. Really, Joe? You stood there and championed a guy who couldn't even complete a sentence without stumbling over his own tongue? Your support was a disgrace, and don't think the American people will forget it. You lost any credibility you had left, and it's a shame to watch someone who once had potential turn into a mouthpiece for mediocrity.

Jake Tapper—oh, how the mighty have fallen. You used to be a respected journalist, but now? Now, you're just another talking head floating in a sea of noise. You defended Biden time and again, glossing over serious issues with a wave of your hand and a dismissive tone. Your job was to ask tough questions, Jake, not to provide cover for a president who clearly wasn't up to the job. You should be ashamed of yourself for failing to hold him accountable. You then compounded your shame by publishing a book admitting the truth about Biden's mental decline—but only after he left office. So you withheld the facts from the public when they really counted—and then you cashed in afterward. Some journalist. Your career should haunt you with the knowledge that you chose to be part of the problem, not the solution.

Now, let's look at *The View*. If there's one place where common sense goes to die, it's that show. Whoopi Goldberg and Joy Behar have made a career out of shouting down dissent and cheering on an administration that left this country in shambles. They always act like they're on some sort of moral high ground, but in reality their support for Biden was nothing short of tragic. They ignored the glaring issues about him, choosing instead to laugh off serious concerns as if they were just jokes. It's a disgrace, and every time they open their mouths, they cheapen the dialogue we need to have as a nation.

And don't even get me started on the late-night comedians. Stephen Colbert and Jimmy Kimmel have turned their platforms into megaphones for the left. They chose to make mild, deflecting jokes about Biden's gaffes and missteps, offering punchlines rather than serious observations about his competency. Except the punchlines were on all of us. While they were busy laughing, we were living with the consequences of a failing presidency. Their complicity in this charade is unforgivable, and they should be reminded of that every time they sit down to tell a joke.

Howard Stern? Oh, don't think I forgot about you. Once a voice of the people, now just another celebrity in the bubble, afraid to step outside the lines of political correctness. You've traded your edge for a seat at the table of the elite, while ignoring the glaring flaws in the administration you supported. It's a shame to watch someone who once stood for free speech turn into a puppet of the establishment.

And let's not skip over George Clooney and Barack Obama. Two men who have wielded their influence like a weapon, defending a presidency riddled with incompetence. Clooney, with his smug Hollywood charm, and Obama, with his smooth-talking charisma—both played their parts in perpetuating the laughable narrative that Biden was somehow fit for the job. Your support of him was a slap in the face to everyone who actually cared about the future of this country. You put your celebrity status above integrity, and that's something that shouldn't be forgotten.

Every one of these figures has made their choice. They decided to ignore reality, to turn a blind eye to the truth, all for the sake of maintaining their own status and power. But let me tell you something: the American people are smarter than they give us credit for. We saw the hypocrisy, the lies, and the cowardice. We knew what was happening, and we won't forget.

When the dust settles, they'll have to live with the consequences of their actions. Their names will be tied to a presidency that has failed spectacularly, and their own legacies will be stained with the ink of denial. They chose the expedient path, the one that allowed them to keep their jobs and their friends in the elite circles, but they sacrificed their integrity, honesty, and reputations in the process.

So, to all of them—Psaki, Scarborough, Tapper, Whoopi, Joy, Colbert, Kimmel, Stern, Clooney, Obama, and every other talking head who defended the Biden administration: don't think for a second that we'll forget what you did. Your dishonesty has been laid bare, and it should haunt you for the rest of your careers and lives. The truth has a way of surfacing, and it has left you standing in reputational ruins of your own making.

We need to hold these people accountable for their words and their actions. We can't let them off the hook because they're celebrities or pundits. They've played roles in the downfall of this country, and it's time we call them out for it. The American people deserve better than their lies and the excuses. We deserve leaders who will stand up and tell the truth, even when it's uncomfortable.

The next time you see these figures on your screens or hear them on your radios, remember this. Remember the choices they made when they stood by a failing administration instead of speaking truth to power. Don't ever take them seriously again. Don't believe a word they say. Because the moment you do is the moment you allow the charade to continue. And we can't afford that anymore.

◆ 48 ◆

RELATIONSHIPS

THE LAST FIVE YEARS HAVE been a whirlwind, right? We've seen a full-on assault on masculinity. Everything that once defined what it meant to be a man has been labeled "toxic," and it's made a lot of us take a hard look in the mirror. We're told we're the problem, that being assertive or confident makes us the bad guy. So many men out there, myself included, are wrestling with their identity, their strengths, and their weaknesses. It's a rough ride, and I'm not about to sugarcoat it.

You start questioning everything. What does it mean to be a man? What does it mean to be a good partner? You think you've got it all figured out, and then society flips the script on you. You've got to keep your head on a swivel, constantly assessing whether you're doing things right. But often, the louder the world shouts, the quieter our own voices become. You start doubting yourself. You wonder if your instincts are wrong. You know, that gut feeling? Yeah, that one. It's harder to trust it when everyone's telling you you're the problem.

Let's talk about relationships for a second. It's a tricky balancing act, trying to figure out when to stand your ground and when to compromise. Every guy knows that feeling of being in a relationship where you're just not sure when to call it quits. You get in these situations where you're constantly second-guessing yourself. You start off thinking about that family unit, the roots you want to plant, the dreams you want to build. But as the honeymoon phase fades and reality sets in, it's like someone flipped a switch. Those rose-colored glasses come off, and suddenly you're staring at a different person across the dinner table.

You think, "This is exciting and new," but then the magic fizzles out, and you're left with the reality of two people just trying to make it work—often without success. And let me tell you, there's nothing wrong with wanting to build something lasting. It's just that sometimes you find yourself in a situation that feels like quicksand. The more you struggle, the deeper you sink.

Things you say silently in your head but can't say out loud echo through your mind: *I know you don't want me; I'm not stupid.* You feel it in their presence, their words are dismissive, their silence is deafening; their look is as bitter as a lemon. Why, as men, do we stay? You hold on to the tiniest shred of hope that she will love you again, that she will tell you you're worth it. You cling to that like a drug addict's first hit. You tell yourself to leave; you deserve better. But you don't leave, because you're dreaming or hoping for that call where she says: I want you; I need you; I'm sorry. It's fool's gold, and deep down, you know you're doing self-harm to your heart.

I've always had this "I can't give up" mentality. Quitting feels like failure. It feels like admitting defeat, and that's something I've never been good at. But you can take that mentality too far. You end up in relationships that are dragging you down, holding you back from being the man you want to be. You're stuck in this cycle of hope and despair, wanting things to get better, but knowing deep down they probably won't. And that's the hard truth: sometimes, things just don't improve.

For men, it's a struggle to open up. You can't call someone and say, *My heart hurts. Why doesn't she want me anymore?* For me, I struggle at times; my mother hasn't been in my life for decades, but there's still a part of me hoping for a call one day saying, *I'm proud of you. I love you. You're a good man, and you're a good son.* The reality is it won't happen, but that torment won't ever go away until she's gone from this earth. Then the hope and the dream die with it. It can be the same with a wife or partner. I've always had a broken heart, but the trade-off is that it made me funny. It's part of my ingredients to becoming me.

As men, it's tough to admit we're in a bad place. We don't want to be vulnerable. We don't want to look weak. You know what I mean? Asking your partner if they're still attracted to you? That feels like stepping off a cliff without a parachute. It's terrifying. You're putting yourself out there in a way that leaves you exposed. And when you're already feeling the weight of the world on your shoulders, the last thing you want is to add more to the load.

But here's where it gets complicated. You can find yourself stuck in a relationship that's draining you, yet you hold on for dear life. You keep thinking, "Maybe things will change. Maybe we can turn this around." But the problem is, you often end up in a state of panic, feeling like you're in a no-win situation. You know you should leave, but something holds you back. It's like you're in a prison of your own making.

In cases where one partner exhibits narcissistic behavior, the dynamics become even more challenging. Narcissists often use a sneaky tactic called "reactive abuse" to mess with their victims and twist the truth. This involves deliberately pushing your buttons with relentless emotional, psychological, or even physical abuse until you snap and react in anger or frustration. Then they swoop in and claim you're unstable, irrational, or even abusive yourself. This is all part of their plan to shift the blame away from them and make you look like the problem.

Once they've got you riled up, they'll take it to the next level with smear campaigns. They selectively share their version of events with others, carefully leaving out the ongoing abuse that led to your reaction. Instead, they paint themselves as the victim and you as the aggressor. This manipulation is deeply hurtful, as it invalidates your experiences and isolates you from others who might believe their false narrative. The abuse gets worse because you're left defending yourself against accusations that stem directly from the torment you've endured. But reactive abuse isn't a reflection of your character. It's a calculated tool that the narcissist uses to maintain control and hide their true self.

The worst feeling for a man is when he tries to have a conversation with his partner about what's hurting him. Instead of listening, his partner gets defensive and flips it on him, making him feel like he's the problem. He just wanted to be heard. He just wanted to feel understood. But instead, he questions whether opening up was a mistake. He goes silent, not because he's fine, but because he's exhausted from feeling unheard. It's not weakness. It's not complaining. It's his heart asking for peace, for respect, and for effort.

A man will stop talking when he feels it doesn't matter, and once he shuts down, it's hard to get him back. Silence for him becomes a protective mechanism. He needs patience, not pressure. Support, not judgment. Listen before he stops trusting. Understand before he lets go. Because when he's done, he's done for good.

And think about the societal expectations placed on men. You're expected to be the provider, the protector, the strong one who never shows weakness. But that's a heavy mantle to bear. When you've spent your whole life trying to beat the odds, it's hard to admit when you're struggling. You're conditioned to think that vulnerability is a sign of weakness, but in reality, it's one of the strongest things a man can do. It takes guts to be honest about your feelings, to say, "I'm not okay," and even harder to walk away from a situation that's not serving you.

But we're all human. We all have emotions, and we all feel pain. It's part of the package. We've got to learn to embrace that vulnerability, to accept that it's okay to not have all the answers. It's okay to admit you're struggling, and it's okay to ask for help. That's not weakness; that's strength.

Now, I know what you're thinking: "But what about loyalty?" Loyalty is a noble quality, but it can also be a double-edged sword. You can be loyal to a fault, sticking around long after you should have walked away. It's easy to fall into that trap, believing that if you just hold on a little longer, things will get better. But sometimes, you have to recognize when it's time to cut your losses and move on.

And it's not just about you. It's about your happiness and your partner's happiness, too. If you're both stuck in a toxic cycle, dragging each other down, what good is that?

Sometimes, the most loving thing you can do is to let go, to free each other from the burden of an unhappy relationship. It's a hard truth, but it's one that needs to be faced.

I think back to the times I've tried to hold on, telling myself that maybe this time would be different. I've stayed in relationships long after I knew I should have left, convincing myself that I could fix things. But the reality is, some things just can't be fixed. You can't change people, and you can't force love where it doesn't exist anymore. That's a hard pill to swallow, but it's the truth.

So how do we break that cycle? How do we learn to recognize when it's time to walk away? It starts with self-awareness. You've got to take a hard look at yourself and your situation. Are you happy? Are your needs being met? Are you both growing together, or are you just going through the motions? Those are the questions you need to ask yourself.

And it's okay to be selfish sometimes. It's okay to put your own happiness first. You can't pour from an empty cup, and if you're not taking care of yourself, you won't be able to take care of anyone else. So, don't be afraid to prioritize your own well-being. It's not selfish; it's necessary.

Now, I'm not saying it's easy. It's tough to let go of something you've invested so much time and energy into. But sometimes, the hardest decisions lead to the best outcomes. You might find that once you let go of what's holding you back, you open yourself up to new opportunities and new experiences. You'll start to see the world in a different light.

And remember the importance of communication. It's crucial in any relationship. If you're feeling unhappy or unfulfilled, speak up. Don't bottle it up inside. You've got to share your feelings, your fears, and your desires. It's not always easy, but it's necessary for growth.

But communication isn't just about talking; it's also about listening. A relationship is a two-way street, and both partners need to feel heard and valued. If you find yourself in a situation where your voice isn't being acknowledged, that's a red flag. It's easy to get caught up in your own feelings and frustrations, but remember, your partner is navigating their own struggles, too.

That brings us back to vulnerability. It's a tough nut to crack. For many men, the idea of being vulnerable feels like stepping off a cliff. But let me tell you, there's power in vulnerability. It opens the door to deeper connections and honest conversations. When you allow yourself to be vulnerable, you invite your partner to do the same. It's a game-changer.

You might be thinking, "But what if they don't reciprocate?" That's a valid concern. But you can't control how someone else responds. You can only control your own actions and reactions. If you're being honest and open, and they're still not meeting you halfway, it might be time to reevaluate the relationship. Remember, you deserve someone who values your feelings and is willing to put in the effort to make things work.

Change is hard. Breaking old patterns takes time and effort. But the first step is recognizing that you're in a cycle that isn't serving you. It's about having the courage to face the truth, even when it's uncomfortable. It's about being willing to let go of the familiar, even when it feels safe, and stepping into the unknown.

And I get it; the fear of the unknown can be paralyzing. You might worry about being alone or about what the future holds. But sometimes the unknown can lead to incredible opportunities. When you let go of what's holding you back, you create space for new possibilities—new relationships, new experiences, and newfound happiness.

So, what's the takeaway here? It's simple: be aware of your worth. Don't settle for less than you deserve, and don't be afraid to walk away from situations that aren't serving you. Embrace vulnerability, communicate openly, and don't forget to prioritize your own happiness. Life's too short to be stuck in a cycle of misery.

In the end, it's all about finding that balance. It's about recognizing when to hold on and when to let go. It's about being a man in today's world while staying true to yourself. And believe me, that's the hardest battle of all. But if you keep pushing forward, keep striving for growth, and keep believing in yourself, you'll emerge stronger, wiser, and ready to take on whatever life throws your way.

Guys, you are not alone. We're all in this together, and together, we can break the cycle and create the lives we want to live. Remember, it's okay to love and to lose, but it's even more important to learn and to grow. That's where the real strength lies.

And as you move forward, keep this in mind: life is a journey, not a destination. Embrace the ups and downs, the twists and turns. Every experience, whether good or bad, shapes who you are. So take it all in, learn from it, and don't be afraid to forge your own path. You've got this.

◆ 49 ◆

THE LAST DAYS OF BOXER—A FISH STORY

IN THE DIM LIGHT OF my aquarium room, the familiar hum of the filters was a constant reminder of the life that thrived within the glass. This was my sanctuary, a space where the chaos of the outside world faded away. But today, a heavy weight settled in my chest as I watched Boxer, my male jaguar cichlid, nearing the end of his life.

Boxer was a tough bastard. I'd brought him home a decade ago, a scrappy little fish barely the size of my thumb. From the moment he swam into my life, he had been a fighter—always the first to challenge the bigger fish and the last to back down. I still remember the day he tried to swallow a catfish, getting himself into serious trouble. The barbs lodged in his gills forced me to wrestle him with pliers, adrenaline pumping through me as I saved his sorry ass. That day forged a bond between us that no one else could understand unless they'd been in the trenches with a fish like him.

But now, at ten years old, Boxer was past his prime. His once-vibrant colors had dulled, and his vision was failing. The other fish had started to bully him, and while I knew this was nature's way of taking its course, I wasn't ready to let him go. I wanted him to leave with dignity, not as a victim of the tank bullies.

When I moved him to a new tank, I checked on him and found him lying on his side, wedged in the corner. My heart sank. Flashbacks hit me like a freight train—memories of feeding him as a tiny fish, the countless hours spent watching him thrive, and the bond we had built over the years. People might think it's crazy to form such a connection to a fish, but they're wrong. We're all living beings, and the bonds we form transcend species. There's no science book that can explain it.

His gills barely moved, just a slow, labored rhythm. Healthy fish breathe continuously, but Boxer was struggling. In that moment, I thought, "This is it. He's going wherever fish go when they die." But then I noticed something that stopped me in my tracks: his female counterpart, whom I had taken to calling "Mama Bear," was hovering protectively over him. Any fish that dared to approach was met with a fierce defense. She was attacking anything that came near. I'd never witnessed anything like it before—fish don't typically protect each other like that.

I reached my hand into the tank, and she took a swipe at me, biting my fingers. It hurt like hell, but it was a reminder of her fierce loyalty. I called Mike, my fish guy from Louisiana, and he was just as amazed. "Bro, I've never seen anything like this," he said. "She's not leaving his side." I couldn't help but think, "That's a real ride-or-die." A lot of people could learn something from her.

So, I decided to stick around. I put on some classical music—an odd choice for fish, sure, but they seemed to enjoy it. I played an opera piece, ironically fitting given its themes of betrayal and love. As I watched Boxer's gills slow down, I reflected on the moments he had shared with me—through the ups and downs of my life, the struggles of being a provider, and the chaos that often came with fame. He had been there through it all, a constant in my world.

In those quiet moments, I realized he was much more than just a fish. He was a reminder of resilience, of standing your ground when the world tries to knock you down. He was a fighter, just like me. And as I sat there, I felt a swell of gratitude. I whispered to him, "Thanks for all the memories, old fella. You've earned your rest."

I went to bed that night, exhausted but at peace. When I woke up the next morning, the first thing I did was head straight for the tank. I expected to find him gone, but there he was—still on his side. "You stubborn bastard," I thought, half-amused and half-frustrated. "Not yet, huh?"

Mama Bear was still right there with him, standing guard. The tank was perfectly divided in half, with her protecting her wounded mate. It was as if she was saying, "I'm not done with you yet." In that moment, I realized maybe, just maybe, Boxer wasn't ready to give up either.

Throughout the day, I kept a close eye on them. Boxer was fighting against the tide of age, refusing to accept defeat. Watching him struggle made me think about my own battles—the pressure to provide for my family, the expectations of fans, and the loneliness that often accompanies success. Fame can be a cruel mistress, and sometimes it feels like you're just lying on your side, waiting for the end. But Boxer wasn't done yet, and neither was I.

As the hours passed, I found myself lost in thought. The sacrifices I had made over the years weighed heavy on my mind. The long hours spent working, the constant grind of trying to stay relevant in a world that moves at lightning speed—it all took its toll. I'd built a career that many would envy, but sometimes I felt like a ghost in my own life, drifting from one obligation to the next, with only my fish to keep me company.

But Boxer was a reminder of fortitude He was a fighter, refusing to give in to age and weakness. As I watched him struggle, I couldn't help but draw parallels to my own life. There were days when I felt like lying down and giving up, where the pressure felt too much to bear. But here was Boxer, stubbornly clinging to life. If he could fight, then so could I.

As night fell, I found myself sitting in front of the tank, watching the pair. Mama Bear continued to hover protectively over Boxer, nudging him gently as if to encourage him to keep fighting. I admired that loyalty. It made me think about my own relationships—how many people would stand by you in your darkest moments? How many would fight for you when you couldn't fight for yourself?

That unwavering love is rare, and it made me realize that there's a difference between companionship and commitment. Mama Bear could have easily swum off to find a younger, flashier mate, but she chose to stay with Boxer. That's real loyalty, and it's something I often wished I had in my own life.

I sat there, contemplating my own journey. The sacrifices I had made, the loneliness that often accompanied success—these were the realities of life. But as I sat there, I felt a sense of clarity. Even in the face of death, there's beauty in the struggle. There's dignity in fighting until the very end.

Boxer was still alive, still kicking, defying the odds. As long as he was hanging on, I wasn't going anywhere either. I'd be right there with him, sharing the journey until the end, just like Mama Bear. Because in this crazy, unforgiving world, sometimes all you need is a little love and a lot of heart to make it through.

Then, in the depths of the night, I noticed Boxer stirring slightly. It was subtle, but it was there. Even in his weakened state, he was still trying to swim, still trying to assert himself in a world that had become increasingly hostile. I felt a surge of pride for my little fighter. Maybe he wasn't done yet after all.

As I leaned in closer, I could see the determination etched on his face, and in that moment, I knew I couldn't give up on him. I thought about how many people in my life had given up on their dreams, their passions, their very selves, simply because the going got tough. Boxer was teaching me a lesson I needed to learn: no matter how bleak things seem, you keep fighting. You don't let life push you around.

I decided to stay up a little longer, just to watch. I wanted to be there for him, to support him in whatever way I could. If he was going to fight, then I was going to fight too. In a world that often felt isolating, I found comfort in the presence of these fish—my little family.

As dawn approached, I felt a sense of peace wash over me. Boxer was still there, still with us. And Mama Bear? She was right by his side, just as she had been since the beginning. In that moment, I understood something profound: love and loyalty don't come with conditions. They're about standing together, no matter the odds.

As the sun began to rise, I couldn't help but smile. Boxer was still fighting, and so was I. Whatever lay ahead, we'd face it together. Because sometimes, amidst the struggles of life, all it takes is a little love and the will to keep going. And in that small tank, surrounded by water, I found a lesson that would stick with me long after the day was done.

Epilogue

In the quiet hours of dawn, he slipped away peacefully, proud and not alone. Momma Bear was by his side until his very last breath, supporting him as he struggled to draw water through his gills, transforming it into precious oxygen. With tears in my eyes, I reflected on the life he had lived, proud to have witnessed his journey and to have given him the kind of existence every creature deserves. Boxer was more than just a fish; he was a pioneer in our small aquatic world, a father who fathered hundreds of tiny ones, each carrying a piece of his indomitable spirit.

For nearly a decade, he fought valiantly to assert his place as the alpha in the tank, a testament to his tenacity and strength. Now, as his heart began to slow and he prepared to leave this world behind, he was comforted by the presence of the one who loved him most. In those final moments, as the darkness started to encroach upon his vision, he could feel her gentle touch, a reminder that he was not alone. When she finally released him, it was as if he was given permission to let go, to embrace the peace that awaited him.

I will miss Boxer dearly.

◆ 50 ◆

THE BELTS OF AMERICA

AS THE PLANE GLIDES THROUGH the sky at 35,000 feet, I gaze out the window, watching the vast expanse of America unfurl like a well-worn wrestling mat. Below me, the landscape is a patchwork quilt of towns, cities, and open spaces—each square a story waiting to be told. I can't help but chuckle at the irony: I was once a guy who slammed bodies in the ring for a living, and now I'm flying high above the nation, reflecting on its essence. Who would've thought?

It feels like just yesterday when I stood on the *Gutfeld!* set, adrenaline pumping, and handed a pro wrestling belt to President Trump. Sure, it was a gimmick, but that belt was more than just a shiny piece of hardware. It was a metaphor for the American spirit—hard-fought, often messy, and sometimes downright ridiculous. But hey, that's what makes us who we are. It's not just about winning; it's about the hustle, the grit, and occasionally, the laughter along the way.

Now, as I look down at the colorful tapestry of America, I see more than just land and buildings. I see belts—the Rust Belt, the Bible Belt, the Cotton Belt, and the Sun Belt. Each one represents a different facet of our nation, a different segment of hardworking Americans living their lives with tenacity and spirit. If you think about it, we've got more belts than a WWE pay-per-view event, and each one is just as important.

Let's start with the Rust Belt. Ah, the Rust Belt—the once-thriving heart of American manufacturing, where factories roared like lions and people worked hard for their piece of the American dream. Now? Well, let's just say it's seen better days. But don't let the silence fool you; those people down there are tougher than a two-dollar steak. They've weathered storms, adapted to change, and kept their heads held high, even when the world tried to knock them down. Politicians, take note: those people deserve to be heard, not just patted on the back during election season.

Then we move to the Bible Belt, a region where faith and community are as intertwined as the laces on your favorite pair of wrestling boots. It's a place where families come together on Sunday mornings, and where the spirit of neighborly love is alive and well. Those folks might seem a bit different from the coastal elites, but let me tell you, they know the value of hard work and standing by one another. And if you think they don't have a sense of humor, try sitting through a Southern Baptist potluck—you'll be laughing until the sweet tea comes out of your nose.

Next up is the Cotton Belt, where farmers toil under the blazing sun. These are the people who grow the food that feeds our nation. They're as reliable as your grandmother's secret apple pie recipe—if they say they'll do something, you can take it to the bank. But their stories often go untold, overshadowed by the latest political scandals. Hey politicians, while you're busy chasing your next headline, remember that those farmers are the backbone of this country. They deserve better representation than the occasional photo op at a county fair.

And there's the Sun Belt, where the weather is as warm as the smiles of the people. This region is a melting pot of cultures, a vibrant mix of traditions that show just how diverse and beautiful America can be. People here are living life to the fullest, soaking up the sun, and welcoming newcomers with open arms. If you want to know what makes America great, look no further than the Sun Belt. It's where the spirit of unity shines brighter than the summer sun.

As I continue my flight, I can't help but think of my recent one-man show tours. Those shows were a whirlwind of laughter, tears, and heartwarming moments. I met veterans who shared their stories of sacrifice, teachers who poured their hearts into their classrooms, and families who found joy in the simple act of being together. Each encounter was a reminder of why I do what I do. It's about connecting with people, understanding their struggles, and amplifying their voices.

But it's not just about me. It's about all of us. The elites up in their ivory towers need to take a moment—just one moment—to look down from their lofty perches and remember the people living their lives below. The kid learning to ride a bike for the first time, the couple stressed about their mortgage, the elderly woman clutching the memories of her late husband. These are the faces behind the headlines, the stories behind the statistics, and they deserve to be acknowledged.

And while we're talking belts, let's not forget the hidden gems of America—the lesser-known regions that deserve their moment in the spotlight. There's the Lead Belt in southeastern Missouri, a district with a long history of mining for lead, where the spirit of tenacity runs deep. It's a place that has faced its share of economic ups and downs but continues to persevere, reminding us that even the toughest of industries can weather the storm.

Then there's the Pine Belt in southern Mississippi, where longleaf pine trees stand tall and proud, symbolizing the strength of the local communities that rely on them. The lumberjacks and craftsmen here are the unsung heroes who keep the wheels of industry turning, all while maintaining a deep connection to the land.

And let's take a detour to the Pretzel Belt in Pennsylvania—a district associated with pretzel and snack food production that has tickled the taste buds of countless Americans. Who knew that delicious, crunchy snacks could symbolize the ingenuity and creativity of local entrepreneurs? The Pretzel Belt may not sound as serious as the others, but it's a testament to the delightful quirks that make our nation unique.

Don't overlook the Rice Belt, where southern states grow the grain that feeds not just our nation but the world. These farmers are the quiet giants of agriculture, toiling in the fields under the hot sun, ensuring that we have meals on our tables. Their stories of dedication and hard work should be celebrated—not just during harvest season but year-round.

Finally, we can't forget the Wheat Belt, spanning the northern midwestern states where most of North America's grain and soybeans are grown. The farmers here are the lifeblood of the breadbasket, feeding families from coast to coast. Their grit and resolve are woven into the very fabric of what it means to be American.

As I peer out the window again, taking in the sprawling suburbs, the bustling cities, and the quiet small towns, I'm reminded of the profound responsibility that comes with my voice. I'm just a FOX commentator and a former wrestler, but I'm committed to fighting for the everyday American. The person who wakes up early, puts in the hours, and dreams of a better life. The people who are the true backbone of this nation.

America is not just a collection of states; it's a collection of stories and struggles. Each belt tells a different story, but together they weave the rich narrative of a nation built on hard work, tenacity, and a healthy dose of humor. And I believe it is our duty—no, our honor—to uphold that narrative and ensure it continues to thrive.

As I prepare to land back home, I'm filled with gratitude for the privilege of being a part of this great nation. I'm ready to continue the journey, to keep fighting for those who may feel overlooked or unheard. Because if there's one thing I've learned, it's that every voice matters. Every story deserves to be told. And every belt—whether it's the Rust Belt or the Bible Belt or the obscure but equally vital Lead or Pretzel Belt—should have a seat at the table of democracy.

So, let's hold our leaders accountable. Let's remind them that they're not above us, but among us. Let's ensure that every voice is heard, every story is told, and that we all wear our belts with pride. Because what it is to be American is not just about winning the belt; it's about lifting each other up, supporting one another, and creating a future where every American can thrive.

As I touch down, I carry with me the stories of those I've met, the laughter shared, and the lessons learned. I'll continue to be an advocate for those who deserve better, and I'll keep fighting to ensure that the spirit of America shines brightly for generations to come.

In the end, it's about more than just a title or a belt; it's about what it is to be part of this incredible nation.

That's what it is, America.

—*Tyrus*

ACKNOWLEDGMENTS

A SPECIAL THANK YOU TO president Donald J. Trump for giving a me an opportunity to sit down with him—something that never in my life would I have thought I would do. It was the president's kindness to my family that will forever be instilled in my mind and heart when I think of him. Thank you Mr. President. #goat

Thanks to the team at Post Hill Press, including Anthony Ziccardi and Caitlin Burdette.

To everyone at Gutfeld!

Producers:
Tom O'Connor
Arash Mosaleh
Ryan Brosky
Chrystie Del Corso
Andre Confuorto
Gene Nelson
Mike Castillo
Patrick Kennedy
Gabby Valenti
Natalie Largey

Writers:
Joe Machi
Joe Devito
Sean Medlock
Dan Kendall

Along of course with Greg Gutfeld, Kat Timpf, Kennedy, Dana Perrino, Harold. Ford, Jr., and Charles Payne.

Shout outs to:
Judge Jeanine Pirro
Billy Corgan
Kevin Nash
Tonga loa
Paul Heyman
John Laurinaitis
Johnny Curtis
Heath Slater
Vasean lasene
Brett Witten
Bill Goldberg
Undertaker
Dustin Rhodes
Trevor Murdoch
Aron Haddad
Austin Idol
Chris Jericho
Glenn Jacobs
Bully Ray
J.R. Kratos

Robert Koffie
Robert Anthony
Koffie Kingston
Jezzie
Brian Myers
Matt Cardona
Mike Knox

And to Chris Epting... "Why, Alfred... whatever do you mean?"

ABOUT THE AUTHOR

TYRUS, A FORMER PROFESSIONAL WRESTLING champion, has transitioned from the ring to the spotlight as a prominent media personality. Known for his charismatic presence, he is a *New York Times* bestselling author whose works blend humor and keen insights into contemporary issues. As a popular contributor on Fox News, Tyrus engages viewers with his unique perspective on politics and current events, showcasing his ability to connect with a diverse audience.

In addition to his television career, Tyrus has cultivated a successful one-man show that tours the country, captivating audiences with his storytelling and comedic flair. His journey from the wrestling world to media stardom reflects his versatility and dedication to entertaining while provoking thought. With a loyal following, Tyrus continues to make an impact in both entertainment and political commentary, appealing to fans who appreciate his blend of wit, wisdom, and common-sense approach to pressing issues.